CW00404788

NOAH

English version by Arthur Wilmurt, with introduction by Michel Saint-Denis. An amusing, dramatic and moving version of Noah's relationship with God and his fellow men. Noah is seen as an old peasant of today, and his family reflect the present-day attitudes of the young.

THE HEREFORD PLAYS

General Editor: E. R. Wood

Maxwell Anderson
Winterset

Robert Ardrey
Thunder Rock

Robert Bolt
A Man for All Seasons
The Tiger and the Horse

Harold Brighouse
Hobson's Choice

Coxe and Chapman
Billy Budd

Gordon Daviot
Dickon

Barry England
Conduct Unbecoming

J. E. Flecker
Hassan

Ruth and Augustus
Goetz
The Heiress

H. Granville-Barker
The Voysey Inheritance

(Ed.) E. Haddon
Three Dramatic Legends

Willis Hall
*The Long and the Short
  and the Tall*

Fritz Hochwälder
The Strong are Lonely

Henrik Ibsen
The Master Builder
An Enemy of the People

D. H. Lawrence
*The Widowing of Mrs
  Holroyd and The
  Daughter-in-Law*

Roger MacDougall
Escapade

Arthur Miller
The Crucible
Death of a Salesman
All My Sons

Bill Naughton
Spring and Port Wine

André Obey
Noah

J. B. Priestley
An Inspector Calls
Time and the Conways
When We are Married

James Saunders
*Next Time I'll Sing to
  You*
A Scent of Flowers

R. C. Sherriff
Journey's End

David Storey
In Celebration

J. M. Synge
*The Playboy of the West-
  ern World and Riders
  to the Sea*

Brandon Thomas
Charley's Aunt

Peter Ustinov
Romanoff and Juliet

John Whiting
Marching Song
Saint's Day
A Penny for a Song
The Devils

Oscar Wilde
*The Importance of Being
  Earnest*

Tennessee Williams
The Glass Menagerie

André Obey

Noah

A PLAY IN FIVE SCENES

English Text by
ARTHUR WILMURT

with an Introduction by
MICHEL SAINT-DENIS

HEINEMANN EDUCATIONAL BOOKS
LONDON

Heinemann Educational Books Ltd

LONDON EDINBURGH MELBOURNE AUCKLAND TORONTO
HONG KONG SINGAPORE KUALA LUMPUR NEW DELHI
NAIROBI JOHANNESBURG LUSAKA IBADAN
KINGSTON

ISBN 0 435 22670 3

FIRST PUBLISHED BY WILLIAM HEINEMANN LTD 1935

First published in the Drama Library 1949
Reprinted 1951, 1953, 1955, 1957, 1959, 1962, 1964, 1965
First published in the Hereford Plays Series 1967
Reprinted 1967, 1968, 1970, 1972, 1973, 1975, 1977

Published by
Heinemann Educational Books Ltd
48 Charles Street, London W1X 8AH
Printed and bound in Great Britain by
Morrison & Gibb Ltd, London and Edinburgh

CHARACTERS

NOAH
MRS NOAH
SHEM
HAM
JAPHETH
NAOMI
SELLA
ADA
THE BEAR
THE LION
THE MONKEY
THE ELEPHANT
THE COW
THE LAMB
THE WOLF
THE TIGER
THE MAN

Noah was first presented by Howard Wydham and Bronson Albery at the New Theatre, London, on Tuesday, 2 July 1935, with the following cast:

NOAH	John Gielgud
MRS NOAH	Marjorie Fielding
SHEM	Harold Young
HAM	Colin Keith-Johnston
JAPHETH	Marius Goring
NAOMI	Ena Burrill
SELLA	Cicely Howland
ADA	Jessica Tandy
THE BEAR	George Devine
THE LION	Harry Andrews
THE MONKEY	Eric Wynn-Owen
THE ELEPHANT	Richard Sheridan
THE COW	Barbara Seymour
THE LAMB	Susan Salaman
THE WOLF	Alec Guinness
THE TIGER	Merula Salaman
THE MAN	George Divine

The play was produced by
MICHEL SAINT-DENIS

INTRODUCTION

André Obey wrote *Noah* during the years 1929 and 1930. How was it that a dramatist, keenly interested in the affairs of his own age, should look to the Bible for his inspiration?

In 1948, Obey began to publish an edition of his complete plays; in his introduction to *Noah*, he writes: 'Since 1940, I have received hundreds of letters, telling me that the world war has given such a topical meaning to the old story of the Flood, that it has become painful, almost cruel, to read; my correspondents go on to wonder that in 1929, a dramatist should have been able to predict the catastrophe of 1939, to foretell the ruins from which were born the spirit of hope, the desire to begin all over again, of which my ancient yet youthful patriarch is the very incarnation. Hard as it is for me to disclaim such a flattering gift of prophecy, I must state quite plainly that never once when writing *Noah* did I feel either my country or the rest of Europe to be on the brink of an abyss, nor did I realize that to climb up the rough dusty sides of that abyss, it would need so much truly biblical courage'.

Nobody reading the play today can fail to be struck by its topicality; it struck us in the same way when we first put on the play in 1931. For at that time, more than ten years after the First World War (in which Obey took part) we had been through experiences which had already shaken our belief in the security of human destiny. In *Noah*, Obey did not claim to have written a biblical play; he took his plot from a great theme, and gave it modern treatment to bring it nearer to us, using methods similar to those of the authors of the medieval mystery and miracle plays, when they made Noah and his wife talk to each other; he gave life and reality to a story which centuries had turned into a legend. The idiom of the play is modern: simple and direct, it is not afraid to risk an anachronism by using slang and by making allusion to ways and even to things which evidently did not exist in biblical times. Noah says, to the animals: 'I'm only an old farmer after all', and in the same speech he says: 'All this happening at once, you know, it's taken me by surprise. It's worn me out, bowled me over' – a very colloquial way to express himself. Noah is then, an old peasant of today, his wife is a nice little woman tied to her home, a poor home, by the cares of looking after a family of five, and as for the children, well, they are just the same as any young people we might meet today – more or less respectful to their parents, always inclined to look upon them as being just a bit behind the times, and knowing quite surely that they will manage a good deal better when they are married; in a hurry to experience life to the full, they fall in love as quickly as possible, and go off on their own the moment the great adventure they have been sharing together is over. But the subject of the play is the great adventure itself, and its interest and amusement lie in seeing how such an ordinary family will behave under such extraordinary conditions: the children revolt against their father, the best of them show themselves to be frivolous, lazy and ungrateful; mother goes off her head, for life on board, with its quarrels and tempests, is too much for an old woman who can't help clinging to dreams of a little kitchen and a garden as she knew them before the flood swallowed them up; Noah alone emerges a finer man from an adventure which he does not attempt to understand; he is content to obey, to follow the commandments of a God whose purpose

escapes him, but whom he fears and in whom he has placed
a blind trust. The end of the play finds Noah quite alone: he
begins to build up again, for such is the law of man; he has
become a hero, but is not aware of his own greatness – a
greatness born of his suffering, his humility and of his complete submission.

When I saw the play performed in Holland, the producer
had used sets built so high that the forest and the ark in Scene
I, the desert surrounding Mount Ararat in Scene V, appeared
enormous – the human beings were dwarfed in comparison;
Noah, especially, seemed like a plaything in the hands of God.

But to return to Obey's introduction: 'Neither in this play,
nor in any of the others which came after it,' he writes, 'did I
bother with an idea of a thesis, of symbolism, or of pointing
a moral. . . . I thought of the stage, and that was enough. My
theory is that a play is a *thing* of the theatre so strictly – and
yet at the same time, so freely-invented for the stage, composed and developed on the stage, subjected to the stage to
such an extent that the life, the reality and the rhythm of the
drama are there before the words which express it: it requires
a language, certainly, but no literature for its own sake.'

In these lines, Obey gives us the secret of an attitude not
very easy to understand for those unfamiliar with the mysteries
of writing for the theatre. To Obey, a play exists in the
author's imagination before he has it written down: the pattern
of the action on the stage, its rhythm, the sequence of events
form a tangible structure in his mind, and the moods and
emotions of his characters are there before the actual text is
on paper. I imagine that a choreographer who writes his own
music must approach his composition in this way, both seeing
and hearing in advance the steps of his dancers and the music
which will bring them to life.

It must be remembered also that, when writing *Noah*, Obey
was working for a definite company of actors whom he had

seen playing in Lyons, and who were to become *La Compagnie des Quinze*.

This company was composed of three experienced actors and a dozen or so young people who for nine years had been working together before performing in the villages of Burgundy, and in large towns both in France and abroad.

What kind of training had these young people received, what kind of plays formed their repertoire?

They had served, so to speak, as subjects for an experiment by that great producer who since 1913 had been bringing fresh ideas to the French theatre – Jacques Copeau. It was he who had endued them with a thirst for inventing new things, and with a sincerity which found itself ill at ease in the French theatre at that time.

Turning his back on the theatre of the rationalists, of the psychologists who had made the stage into either a platform for discussing political, social and even medical problems, or into a laboratory for the study of special cases, Copeau had begun by putting a company of professional actors through the classical school, laying particular stress on Molière and Shakespeare. But he soon discovered that classical discipline alone was not enough to break experienced actors of their conventional habits. So he tried out new methods on a group of young people which he specially picked out for the purpose: it was not now a question of instruction, but rather of a search for the truth, in which master and pupils shared, and which the pupils, away from the influence of their master, were one day to pursue even further than he had.

The most important thing was to find out what attitude, what imaginative and physical training were needed to enable a group of actors to invent a simple dramatic sequence and to bring it to life on the stage, without having a text set down for them: the stage must be given back to the actors and to their guide, the producer, so that together they could find ways of portraying life by actions; the force and significance of gesture and of voice must be realized by the actors, while the dramatic action must get back its rhythm, its musical and choreographic quality. The author would be barred from this experimental stage until such time when the research team, having forged a method to bring their ideas to reality, had given shows, whose style would perhaps incite some writer to join the group and to work in strict collaboration with it.

Right in the country, in a tiny village of Burgundy, the chosen company retired to put their dangerous ideas into practice, after four years of preparatory work in Paris.

Every morning, beginning at nine o'clock, in a big open shed, which had been used for making wine, one could see a dozen young people busy at gym, fencing, and acrobatics. An hour later, rehearsals began: under the direction of one of the group, the actors prepared a mime on a given theme; for example, inspired by memories of 1914, they would show a French village, quiet and prosperous, where the daily round of activities would be going on: suddenly comes a noise, followed by an alarm bell, the beating of drums – declaration of war – men at the front – the ups and downs of the battle – women doing men's work – the war nearly lost – the final effort, and victory – the joys of the armistice, then the return of the survivors to their families.

This young company, of which I was a member, was trying to find the means of representing dramatically a vast theme of this kind, relying entirely on mime, rhythm, noises and music.

At first, the country people regarded us with suspicion, but as we accompanied our experimenting with regular visits to the villages, giving performances of the plays of La Fontaine and Molière, and some of the old farces, we were soon known throughout the district and accepted by everybody.

One day in 1927, we were asked by the authorities of

Nuits St Georges to organize a show to celebrate the end of
the wine harvest, and the safe gathering in of the crops.

We decided to put our experiment to the test in front of
an audience; we would act, by mime, dancing and singing,
by monologue and dialogue, the life of the men of the vine-
yards, the *vignerons*, from the beginning of spring to the first
approach of winter. In particular, we mimed their work, for
we had studied it in minute detail. At times, our mime would
be accompanied by a song, or it would take on such a strong
rhythm that we could only express it with a dance: we had
one very strict rule – never to resort to gestures or movements
of which the meaning was not absolutely clear: neither the
action nor the words ever became abstract. From time to
time, to break the monotony of the general effect, we would
introduce a love scene, or perhaps a character would talk
directly to the audience – a *vigneron* would tell of the crop, of
the joys and tribulations of his trade.

We gave this show to two thousand *vignerons*, both owners
and labourers. For two hours, we felt completely at one with
the spectators, who told us that they would never have
believed that their daily toil could be so enjoyable to watch,
and yet they kept repeating: 'But that's exactly as it is, that's
just what does happen.'

This may give you some idea of the company which Obey
was to meet two years later.

He found fifteen actors, whose four years' training and five
years' practical experience had moulded to that type of acting
which did not lend itself easily to complex psychology, but
which was able to animate a broadly-treated general theme.
We were actors capable of showing life rather than explaining
it, relying more on sound and physical movement than on
talking, used to singing and dancing, able to build up from
choral work to the invention of simple, clearly defined
characters.

Admittedly, we had two or three experienced actors with us, but our principal virtue lay in our concerted strength; we were a team whose members were as used to acting together as they were used to living together: we were in fact a chorus, wonderfully united and trained.

Now do you see the connection between this company and the play called *Noah*? Can you deduce from it the right way to produce *Noah* if you want to respect the spirit in which it was written?

The play centres on the unique character of Noah himself. It needs a very good actor for this part – a man with weight and breath, for it is an exacting and tiring role which calls for generosity, friendliness and power: at times, as if almost in spite of himself, Noah attains greatness and authority. Then Mrs Noah – however self-effacing she may be, her part demands a sensitive actress of wit and personality.

Apart from these characters, the play makes use of two choruses: a chorus of children, and a chorus of animals. True, Ham is wicked and Shem lazy, Ada is natural and sincere, whereas Naomi is vain and seductive: in the same way, the cow in her clumsy fashion differs from the tiger with his rather alarming affection; these differences certainly count, but the important thing to remember in producing *Noah* is to make the children and animals act as choruses. There is nothing complex about their individual psychology – it is the movements which they do together which must be thought out and combined so that they give shape and rhythm to the action. For example, it is through their movements together that the children mime the rain as it begins to fall, that they make us feel the roll of the boat during the storm and mutiny of the fourth scene, that they enable us to follow the flight of the dove in the sky; and finally, before going their separate ways, it is together they first set foot on dry land and fight to possess it. In all these scenes, the lines which the chorus speak are there simply to provoke the action; the text is like music, and one must find the right tone and tempo to give it its full value.

When I produced the play for the first time in English, in 1934, with John Gielgud as Noah, I wanted to give the play by the sets and lighting I used, a size and an importance which were probably out of proportion to it. Today, I am convinced that *Noah* does not lend itself to a spectacular production: its greatness lies in its simplicity, and, providing that the actors play their parts with the sincerity and conviction the story demands, there is no need for elaborate lighting and scenery.

We played *Noah* on all the principal stages of Europe, where every possible modern technical device was put at our disposal. Then one day, in the middle of summer, we were invited to perform the play in the open air, in a large park near Nancy. We built ourselves a platform under a big oak tree, at the foot of a sloping lawn. The performance began at three o'clock in the afternoon, and finished at six. The sun behind the spectators was our only spot-light: as the play took its course, so the sun travelled slowly across the heavens to its setting. For scenery, we had the sky and the trees, in the midst of which we had put a ladder, a tent and one or two stools, roughly put together. The old Bible story has never touched the hearts of a present-day audience so surely as it did in this natural setting.

SCENE ONE

A glade. The Ark is at the right, only the poop deck showing, with a ladder to the ground. NOAH *is taking measurements and singing a little song. He scratches his head and goes over the measurements again. Then he calls:*

NOAH (*softly*): Lord . . . (*Louder.*) Lord . . . (*Very loud.*) Lord! . . . Yes, Lord, it's me. Extremely sorry to bother You again, but . . . What's that? Yes, I know You've other things to think of, but after I've once shoved off, won't it be a little late? . . . Oh, no, Lord, no, no, no. . . . No, Lord, please don't think that. . . . Oh, but naturally, of course, I trust You! You could tell me to set sail on a plank – a branch – on just a cabbage leaf. . . . Yes, You could even tell me to put out to sea with nothing but my loincloth, even without my loincloth – completely — (*He has gone down on his knees, but he gets up immediately.*) Yes, yes, Lord, I beg Your pardon. I know Your time is precious. Well, this is all I wanted to ask You: Should I make a rudder? I say, a rudder. . . . No, no, Lord. R for Robert; U for Una; D for . . . that's it, a rudder. Good . . . very good, I never thought of that. Of course, winds, currents, tides . . . What was that, Lord? Storms? Oh, and while You're there just one other little thing. . . . Are You listening, Lord? (*To the audience.*) Gone!! . . . He's in a bad temper. . . . Well, you can't blame Him; He has so much to think of. All right; no rudder. (*He considers the ark.*) Tides, currents, winds. (*He imitates the winds.*) Psch! . . . Psch! . . . Storms. (*He imitates the tempests.*)

1

Vloum! Be da Bloum! Oh, that's going to be (*he makes a quick movement*) simply . . . magnificent!! . . . No, no, Lord, I'm not afraid. I know that You'll be with me. I was only trying to imagine. . . . Oh, Lord, while You're there I'd like just to ask . . . (*To the audience.*) Che! Gone again. You see how careful you have to be. (*He laughs.*) He was listening all the time. (*He goes to the Ark.*) Storms! . . . I think I'll just put a few more nails in down here. (*He hammers and sings.*)

> When the boat goes well, all goes well.
> When all goes well, the boat goes well.

(*He admires his work.*) And when I think that a year ago I couldn't hammer a nail without hitting my thumb. That's pretty good, if I do say so myself. (*He climbs aboard the Ark and stands there like a captain.*) Larboard and starboard! . . . Cast off the hawsers! . . . Close the portholes! . . 'Ware shoals! . . . Wait till the squall's over! . . . Now I'm ready, completely ready, absolutely ready! I'm ready. (*He cries to Heaven.*) I am ready! (*Then quietly.*) Well, I should like to know how all this business is going to begin. (*He looks all around, at the trees, the bushes, and the sky.*) Magnificent weather – oppressively hot and no sign of a cloud. Well, that part of the programme is His look-out.

Enter the BEAR.

Well! . . . What does *he* want?

The BEAR *moves towards the Ark.*

Just a minute, there!

The BEAR *makes a pass at the Ark.*

(*Frightened.*) Stop that. (*Pulls up ladder.*)

The BEAR *stops.*

Sit down! Good.

BEAR *sits.*

Lie down.

BEAR *lies down on its back and waves its legs gently.*

There's a good doggie.

Enter the LION.

What the devil!

The LION *puts its paw on the Ark.*

None of that, you! . . . Lie down.

The LION *lies down beside the* BEAR.

Fine! . . . Splendid! . . . Now what do they want? Besides, why don't they fight? (*To the animals.*) Hey! Why aren't you fighting? Come on, there. Boo! Woof!

The BEAR *and the* LION *get up and sniff at each other sociably.*

Whoever heard of wild animals behaving like that?

Enter the MONKEY.

Another one! . . . It's a zoo. . . . Sit down, monkey, sit down. Now, look here, my pets, here have I been working every day for a whole year and not one of you has ever shown me the tip of his nose before. Are you out to make trouble for me now that I've finished my work? Come, you can't mean that, surely. (*He thinks it over.*) Unless . . . Oh! But that makes all the difference. Lord! Lord! (*Between his teeth.*) Not there as usual.

Enter the ELEPHANT.

Get back there, Jumbo! No pushing out of turn.

The ELEPHANT *salutes him.*

Good morning, old fellow. Now, if I understand you rightly, you want to come on board, eh?

The animals move forward.

Stop! I didn't say you could! . . . Well. All right, I'll let you come aboard. Yes, I don't see what I can. . . . No, I don't see anything against it. (*He sighs deeply.*) So the time has come! All right. Up with you!

Enter the COW, *gambolling.*

Gently there, gently . . . (*He taps the* COW *on the rump.*)

Wait a minute. Don't I know you? Aren't you that old cow from Mordecai's herd?

The COW *moos gaily.*

Bless my soul! (*With feeling.*) And He picked on you! . . . (*To the* BEAR.) Well, my friend, will you make up your mind?

The BEAR *sniffs the ground, but he doesn't advance.*

What's the matter, old boy? (NOAH *puts on his spectacles and leans over the spot where the bear is sniffing.*) What? Afraid of that insect? An ant! Ha, ha, ha! A bear afraid of an ant. Ha, ha, ha! (*But suddenly he strikes his brow.*) Oh! but what a fool I am! Why it's not an ant, it's *the* ant! It got here first, and I never saw it. Lord! What marvels there are on the threshold of this new life. It will take a stout heart, a steady hand, and a clear eye! I think my heart is right, but my eyes are dim . . . my hands are trembling . . . my feet are heavy. . . . Ah, well, if You've chosen me, perhaps it's because I am, like her – the least wicked of the herd. Come, all aboard. Make yourselves at home.

The animals go into the Ark.

Straight ahead, across the deck! Down the stairway to the left. You'll find your cabins ready. They may look like cages, but they'll be open always. (*He turns towards the forest.*) Come on, all of you! Hurry, you lazybones, you slow-coaches, creepy crawlers; you who travel in herds and you who walk alone – mustangs, mastadons, jabberwocks and unicorns, cloven hoofs and crumpled horns! Hurry! Every one! Everyone! (*He catches his breath.*) Ah, ha! Here come the wolf and the lamb, side by side.

The WOLF *and the* LAMB *enter and go into the Ark.*

Here are the frog and the bull. . . . The fox and the crow. . . . And the birds! What are they waiting for? Come, my little ones. Come! Come!

The singing of the birds begins.

Look. The hare and the tortoise! Come on. Come on. Hurrah! The hare wins! Things are getting back to normal! Ah, this will be the golden age!

A great concert of birds. NOAH *falls on his knees. A pause. Then the* TIGER *enters behind* NOAH. *He goes to* NOAH *and taps him on the shoulder. The birds are suddenly still.*

(*Terrified.*) Ooooo! (*He rises to flee.*) I know you wouldn't hurt me; it's just the surprise, you know. I'm not a bit afraid. . . . (*His teeth are chattering.*) I'm not afraid a bit. It's not me. It's just that my feet have gone cold! It'll soon pass. Wait a minute! They are still cold.

The TIGER *creeps towards him.*

Perhaps, if I do this. . . . (*He turns his back and covers his ears.*) Go on, get aboard! Hurry up.

The TIGER, *with one bound, leaps aboard the Ark.*

Are you still there?

Roaring from the Ark.

Good! (NOAH *turns around and wipes his brow.*) Phew!

Off stage is heard the voice of a boy. It is JAPHETH.

JAPHETH: Whoo-hoo! Father!

NOAH: Ah, here comes the children. . . . Whoo-hoo!

JAPHETH (*nearer*): Whoo-hoo!

NOAH: Whoo-hoo!

VOICE OF SHEM: Look here, Japheth. We agreed; no running. Stick to the rules, or I won't play.

JAPHETH (*entering. He is seventeen*): I'm not running. Morning, Dad! (*He goes to* NOAH *in great strides.*)

SHEM (*entering. He is twenty-one*): You are running! Isn't he, Father?

JAPHETH (*throws himself into* NOAH'S *arms*): Home! I told you my way was shorter.

SHEM: If you're going to run the whole way. . . . Hello, Father.

NOAH (*embracing them both*): Good morning, children. You

both win; Japheth got here first, but he cheated a little. Well, my big sons, did you have much difficulty finding where I was?

JAPHETH: Hoho, Dad! So this is where you've been coming every day. Come on, tell us about it.

NOAH: Just a minute.

Enter HAM. *He is nineteen.*

SHEM and JAPHETH: We beat you!

HAM: All right, all right.

SHEM and JAPHETH: We won!

HAM: All right! (*He goes to* NOAH.) Good morning, Father.

NOAH (*embracing him*): Hello, Ham, my boy. (*To the three of* them.) Where is your mother?

HAM: She's coming.

NOAH: One of you might have waited for her.

    HAM *wanders over to the Ark.*

JAPHETH: She didn't want us to. She said she'd get along better alone. Then she can puff as much as she likes.

NOAH: You can both go back some of the way and meet her.

SHEM (*lying on the ground*): Aw, Father, it's so hot.

JAPHETH: Come on, we'll take it slowly.

SHEM (*getting up*): Oh, what a bore!

JAPHETH (*pointing to the Ark*): New house?

NOAH: Ssshh!

JAPHETH: It's nice.

NOAH: Isn't it?

    SHEM *and* JAPHETH *go out.* HAM *is examining the Ark, his hands behind his back.* NOAH *goes to him and takes his arm.*

Well, son, what do you think of it?

HAM: That?

NOAH: Why, yes.

HAM: What is it?

NOAH: Can't you guess? Is it such a funny shape?

HAM: Hm! It's hard to say. Come on, Father, what is it exactly?

NOAH: It's . . . well, it's made of cypress. It's all cypress. And it's . . . it's coated with pitch, inside and out.

HAM: Like a boat?

NOAH: Like a . . . yes. Hm! And it's three hundred cubits long and fifty cubits wide and thirty cubits high . . .

HAM: But that's ten times too big for us.

NOAH: It's . . . yes it's pretty big. But does it . . . look like *anything*?

HAM: It's not bad . . . not bad, but why the devil build a house like a boat?

NOAH: Ah! It does look like a . . . ?

HAM: Exactly.

NOAH: Listen. (*His tone changes.*) Who knows what will happen? Suppose there was a great flood. . . .

HAM (*laughing*): Here?

NOAH: A . . . tidal wave. . . .

HAM: In this part of the world?

NOAH: A deluge. . . .

> *A noise is heard off.*

(*To* HAM): Ssshh!

> *Enter* SHEM *and* JAPHETH, *carrying their* MOTHER *on their crossed arms and singing:* 'Here is Mamma. Look at Mamma. See who is bringing in darling Mamma.'

SHEM and JAPHETH:
Here is Mamma.
Look at Mamma.
See who is bringing in darling Mamma.

> NOAH *begins to laugh.* SHEM *and* JAPHETH *seat* MAMMA *on the grass and dance around her.*

HAM: Oh, don't make such a row!

NOAH: Good morning, old lady, good morning! (*He kisses her.*)

MAMMA (*panting*): Phew! Phew!

NOAH: Tired, eh?

MAMMA: It's so terribly hot. (*To* JAPHETH.) Oh, did you lock the door carefully?

JAPHETH: Why . . . er . . . yes.

MAMMA: You didn't at all.

JAPHETH: I did, but . . . I think I left the key in the lock.

MAMMA: We must get it out at once. Run back to the house —

JAPHETH: Oh, I say look here! . . .

MAMMA: Go on, run!

NOAH: No, you stay here! (*To* MAMMA.) I'm sorry, Mother, but it's no use getting the key.

MAMMA: No use! . . . What, with neighbours like ours?

NOAH: Well . . . I had a nice little speech in my head explaining everything, but now I don't know quite how to tell you. . . . My dear wife, my darling children, we're never going back to our house. . . . There!

A short pause.

THE THREE BOYS: What?

MAMMA: For months I've felt that there was something worrying you. Why don't you tell me about it? You know I always understand.

HAM: Father always likes a mystery.

NOAH: Don't be so silly.

HAM: All right, but you must admit that we might have been consulted. People don't build houses out in the middle of a forest miles from everybody, and everything. Why, just to get provisions it'll take two hours, there and back.

NOAH: Be quiet.

HAM: Suppose mother forgets the bread . . . and that has been known to happen. . . .

NOAH (*laughing bitterly*): Bread! Ha, ha, ha! bread. . . .

HAM: We'll need it, won't we? Aren't we going to eat any more?

NOAH: Be quiet, do you hear? Quiet!

MAMMA: Now stop it, both of you, stop it! All right, dear, we're not going home any more. That's that. You've told us the worst, I suppose.

JAPHETH: And I don't see that it's so terrible. This house looks much nicer than the old one. Doesn't it, Shem?

SHEM (*practically asleep*): Hmmmm?

JAPHETH: You see, he isn't losing any sleep over it.

JAPHETH *and* MAMMA *have a good laugh.*

NOAH: How sweet of you! How sweet of you both to take it like this.

MAMMA: We are very fond of you, that's all. It isn't hard to be fond of someone like you. Now finish your story and we'll go and see our new house.

NOAH (*in a low voice*): It isn't a house.

JAPHETH and MAMMA: What?

JAPHETH (*nudging* SHEM): Listen to this, you.

NOAH: It's not a house.

SHEM: What is it?

NOAH: It's a ship.

MAMMA and THE BOYS: A what?

NOAH: A ship.

JAPHETH: Splendid!

HAM: Nonsense!

SHEM (*sitting up*): Honest Injun?

MAMMA: A ship!

JAPHETH: Didn't I tell you? Shem, what did I tell you? It's a boat.

SHEM: Can we go on board?

NOAH: Not without me. Admire it from here.

HAM: That's right. Wait.

The two boys go behind the Ark.

SHEM: What shall we call it?

MAMMA: A ship. . . .

HAM: What on earth for?

NOAH: Well . . . er . . . for going sailing.

HAM: Sailing! But on what?

NOAH: God will provide, my son.

HAM: Oh, come now, Father. Let's be serious!

NOAH: We're going sailing. Yes . . . we're going on a little trip.

MAMMA: But you hate trips.

NOAH: Oh, no, no! One can change one's mind sometimes, you know. We'll be nice and quiet, all by ourselves. We won't see another soul. People are pretty unbearable nowadays, don't you think? Wicked! Coarse! Hateful! A bit of solitude with nothing but sea and sky will do us a world of good, it will give us new ideas. And when we get back . . . (*In a low voice.*) When we get back . . .

HAM: But, my dear Father, here we are living in the middle of such a terrible drought that we've almost forgotten what water's like, hundreds of miles from the sea, with every stream and river as dry as a bone, and you, who've been a farmer all your life, suddenly choose this moment to want to be a sailor.

NOAH: No, it isn't that, a bit. I don't feel that at all.

MAMMA (*tenderly*): Tell us, Noah. There's something on your mind, I'm sure. Tell us about it.

HAM: Yes, for heaven's sake, tell us.

VOICE OF JAPHETH (*off stage*): Why, this is wonderful!

VOICE OF SHEM: You bet it is. This is great!

NOAH: Come on, let's go and join them. (*He helps* MAMMA *to her feet.*) It will do us good to hear them laugh.

HAM: But, Father. . . .

JAPHETH (*appearing*): Papa! What's that gadget with the rope . . .!

NOAH: Gadget? Rope! Which one. There are plenty of gadgets and ropes.

JAPHETH: The one with the two pulleys in front; a big one and a little one, for lifting machinery.

NOAH: Ah, yes.

JAPHETH: Well, it's a stroke of genius! Come and see it, Ham.

HAM: All right! What's the hurry?

JAPHETH: You're a genius, Father.

SHEM (*appearing*): Japheth, come and see the sliding panel. Father, you're an ace! Mother, your husband's an ace!

MAMMA: I don't doubt it for a minute.

JAPHETH: But, Father, how did you ever invent it?

NOAH: I'll tell you. Have you ever noticed that when a wood-cutter wants to lift a tree-trunk . . . the way he rolls up his rope . . .

> *They go out.*

HAM (*following them*): Crazy!

> *Their voices die away.*

> *Enter from back three girls:* ADA, SELLA, *and* NAOMI.

ADA: Come, girls, follow the cat. Don't lose it. I feel we must follow the cat.

SELLA: And *I* think it's getting us lost. We've never been so far into the forest.

NAOMI: Besides, we've lost it.

ADA: Then we must look for it. We've got to find it. Hunt for it, sisters, hunt for it! (*She calls.*) Kitty! Kitty!

SELLA and NAOMI: Kitty, Kitty, Kitty!

> *They make the little lip-noise which calls cats.*

ADA: There it is. Look at its little white tail sliding through the grass. Come on, come on!

NAOMI: I can't go any further. It's so hot!

> *They see the Ark.*

ADA: Look! A woodcutter's house.

SELLA: Huh. What a funny-looking house.

NAOMI: Ada, I'm afraid you've led us into some kind of danger.

ADA: We must go into that house.

SELLA (*frightened*): Oh, no!

NAOMI: No, no!

SELLA: Please, let's go back!

NAOMI: Yes! Yes, let's try to find the road back to the village.

   MRS NOAH'S *voice off*. Kitty, Kitty.

ADA: Be quiet. Listen.

VOICE OF MAMMA: Oh, look! The cat! Noah! Noah! Look at the cat!

JAPHETH: Kitty!

NOAH: Kitty!

SHEM: Well, if it isn't dear old Kitty!

ADA: What did I tell you? (*She calls.*) Mrs Noah!

THE THREE GIRLS: Mrs Noah!

   MAMMA *enters*.

MAMMA: What's this? You here, my pretties? (*She calls off stage.*) Shem! Ham! Japheth! Come and see your friends. (*To the girls.*) What brought you here?

ADA (*wrapping her arms about* MAMMA'S *neck*): Oh, Mrs Noah. Dear Mrs Noah!

MAMMA: There, there. What's the matter?

SELLA: She's been excited all morning.

   Three boys enter.

NAOMI: Yes. She couldn't stay still. She burst into tears for no reason at all.

SELLA: She never stopped talking about you.

NAOMI: She wanted to go to your house. She wanted to see you. She insisted on seeing you.

ADA: Dear Mrs Noah! (*To her sisters.*) We've just escaped a great danger.

NOAH (*enters above Ark*): How do you know, little one?

ADA: I . . . I feel it. (*She goes and kneels before* NOAH.) I'm *sure* of it.

NOAH *lifts her up, gazes at her, presses her to him, and raises his eyes up to heaven. A short silence.*

THE THREE BOYS (*in a low voice, but joyously*): Good morning!

NAOMI and SELLA: Good morning!

JAPHETH: Are you sailing with us?

SELLA and NAOMI: What?

SHEM: You know, you'd make pretty little cabin-boys.

SELLA and NAOMI: Pretty . . . *what*?

HAM: If we have to draw lots to see who's to be eaten, I hope the lot falls on Naomi. She's so nice and brown. I'll take a wing, please.

MAMMA *and the boys laugh.*

NAOMI: What are you talking about?

More laughter.

NOAH (*coming back to earth*): Yes, you have indeed escaped a great danger. (*A pause; then joyously.*) Why on earth didn't I think of it before? We have three lovely neighbours. . . . Orphans, if you please. They share our life with us. We say our prayers together. We talk across the fence. And I – I forgot all about them! Now, isn't it lucky that. . . . But how did you happen to meet the cat?

ADA: She was over in your house . . .

MAMMA: Oh, you've been to our house?

ADA: Yes.

SELLA: Yes. Do you know there were a lot of people waiting outside.

NOAH: Aha.

NAOMI: Oh, yes, a whole crowd. Men and women and children from the village. And some men from other villages, too. And they were all whispering and waving their arms.

NOAH: Ah! We were just in time! . . . Go on.

SELLA: All of a sudden Ada cried out, 'Come with me.'

NAOMI: She took each of us by the hand and led us out of doors.

SELLA: We went through the crowd —

NAOMI: We found ourselves at your gate.

ADA: I pulled away a man who was listening at the door. I went in —

MAMMA: Japheth, the key!

ADA: Nobody was there.

SELLA: Except the cat.

ADA: Except the cat. She rubbed herself against my legs and meowed enough to break your heart.

MAMMA: Poor Kitty!

ADA: We came out again . . .

SELLA: That is, we wanted to get out, but the crowd was so thick —

NAOMI: It was like a wall of faces across the door . . .

JAPHETH: Meow!

SELLA: She arched her back —

NAOMI: She spat like mad —

ADA: And the crowd backed away.

The three boys laugh.

ADA: So we went through. We followed the cat and she led us into the forest.

THE BOYS: Ah!

SELLA: Every now and then she turned around to see if we were following.

THE BOYS: Oh!

NAOMI: We lost her!

THE BOYS: Och!

ADA: We found her again!

THE BOYS: Whee!

ADA, SELLA and NAOMI: And here we are!

THE BOYS: Hurray!

General embraces.

HAM (*to* NOAH): Now, are you going to explain?

NOAH (*his voice vibrating*): Yes!

ALL: Ah!

NOAH: I'll tell you everything. It's a great secret, a terrible secret. It has been vexing my heart and preying on my mind for months . . . for a whole year . . . I had no right to trouble you with it before. But now . . . today . . .

JAPHETH: Sshh!

NOAH: Eh!

JAPHETH (*in a low voice*): Someone's hiding just over there!

ALL: Where?

JAPHETH: Sshh! There. (*He points.*) In the bushes.

Something whistles over the stage.

THE THREE BOYS: An arrow!

NOAH: Women to the back!

MAMMA and the girls retreat towards the Ark.

Another whistling.

THE BOYS: Another!

NOAH: To the ship!

All move towards the Ark. A shout off stage. Then a MAN, a sort of hunter, with a savage face, runs in, stops short, plants himself firmly, points a spear at NOAH.

THE MAN: Stop! . . . Stop! . . . Stop! (*To the girls who are moving up ladder.*) Well, you fillies, are you deaf? One move and I skewer the old boy to the wall.

JAPHETH (*trying to drag his brothers*): Come on! Let's go for him!

MAMMA: Don't move.

MAN (*to* JAPHETH): If you are looking for trouble, cocky . . .

NOAH: Steady, Japheth, steady. He'll kill you.

MAN: You bet I will!

MAMMA and THE CHILDREN: Scoundrel! Ruffian!

NOAH: Silence.

Mutterings from the youngsters.

Now, that's enough! (*To the* MAN.) Don't keep on waving
that thing about. Your arm will get tired.

MAN: I seen you. I seen you! You sorcerer. Talking to the
animals. Pinching a cow from Mordecai. Playing with bears
and lions and tigers, not to mention elephants. I seen you!
The whole village is going to know. I'll tell them. Sorcerer!
Sorcerer!

THE THREE BOYS: Stop it!

MAN: It's none of your business. All you've got to do is keep
your mouth shut. What's more, the animals are in there!
(*He points to the Ark.*) I've seen 'em coming. That's where
they are . . . in there!

   MAMMA *and the youngsters laugh. The* MAN *rushes to
the ark and beats on it with his fist. Roaring from the
animals.*

MAMMA and THE YOUNGSTERS (*frightened*): Oh!

MAN: Hahaha! Who's laughing now? Ah, he looks gentle
enough, but he's up to plenty of tricks behind your back!
He's bad. He never could make anything with his hands
before that. (*Pointing to Ark.*) He's a menace to the whole
country.

MAMMA: Be quiet!

MAN: Listen, I'll tell you something. This drought that's been
roasting us for three months, that nobody's never seen nothing like before, that'll knock us all dead with our mouths
open this winter . . . that's him. He done it! He's the one
that done it.

NOAH: Are you sure you're quite all right in the head?

MAN: You done it! There! We all got together! We took a
vote. And we all voted alike – unanimous – that it's all your
fault.

NOAH: Oh, well, in that case . . .

MAN: Listen! I represent the community, so to speak. The
head man says to me, 'Watch that old bird,' he says. 'He

acts stupid, but he knows all the tricks.' Everything that's gone wrong . . . he started it.

MAMMA: Oh, Noah, if they think that, that's terrible!

NOAH: Ssshh! Ssshh!

MAN: I seen you! You look up in the air like this. (*He imitates* NOAH *praying.*) And straight away it gets hotter, and hotter. I seen you doing your abracadabra. And then the sky opens like an oven door, and the oven is white hot, and the ground where I was lying was like a gridiron.

YOUNGSTERS (*in a low voice*): Oh!

MAN: All right, now you got to pay for it. Yes, you've got to come with me. But I don't need the whole issue. The head'll do. (*He leaps towards* NOAH.)

   MAMMA *and the girls scream. The boys line up in front of* NOAH.

NOAH: You wretched creature! (*He steps in front of them all and smiles. A pause.*) This drought — (*He half turns towards his family.*) . . . He hoped it would make them see; that they'd say to themselves, 'It must be. It's a judgment from heaven.' I told them so myself, in every possible way. They laughed in my face. They spat on me. They threw stones at me.

MAMMA and THE YOUNGSTERS: Yes.

NOAH: Didn't I tell them often enough?

MAMMA and THE YOUNGSTERS: Oh, yes.

NOAH: I told them again and again, didn't I?

MAMMA and THE YOUNGSTERS: Oh yes, yes, yes.

NOAH (*turning towards the* MAN): Fool! To think they're all like you. Idle, greedy, thieving, wicked!

   MAN *sneers.*

And on top of that, sneering and sniggering at everything!

MAN: Aw, you old fool. You old idiot.

NOAH (*walking up to him*): Tell me, my friend, can you swim?

MAN: What?

NOAH: I asked if you could swim.

MAN: Aw, come on! None of your tricks with me. I know you.

NOAH: Once and for all, yes or no. Can you swim?

MAN: Of course.

NOAH: Can you swim for a long time?

MAN: You bet!

NOAH: You'll have to swim a long time . . . So long that it might be better if you couldn't swim at all. Then it would be over sooner.

MAN: Over?

NOAH: Yes, over. That's what I said – finished.

MAN: What's going to be finished?

NOAH: Everything! You. Your friends. Your relations. The village. All the villages. This forest. All the forests, all the animals, all human beings in the water! Under the water! With your sins like stones around your neck.

MAN (*bending double*): Hahahahaha!

NOAH (*bending double too*): Hahahahahaha!

MAN: Hahahahahaha!

NOAH: It's going to rain. Rain! You hear what I say? . . . *Rain!*

The MAN, *the children, and* MAMMA *raise their eyes to the sky.*

MAN: Hahahahahaha!

HAM (*to* SHEM, *under his breath*): Has Father got a touch of the sun? There's not a cloud in the sky!

NOAH: Such rain as has never been before. Pouring, drenching, spouting rain. Water swirling, water roaring – hurricanes sweeping madly across the sky – tattered clouds streaming out like great black flags ripped by lightning. Fish will play in the trees. On the tops of mountains, where there were soaring eagles, there will be ravening sharks. And the bodies of the drowned with arms outstretched, rolling over and over, down and down and down. He told me.

MAN: Who?

NOAH: God.

MAN: Who's that?

NOAH: God!

MAN: Oh, of course!

NOAH (*louder*): God.

MAN: Try again.

NOAH (*very loud*): Almighty God!

> MAMMA *and the children drop to their knees.*

MAN: Hahahaha! (*He stutters with glee.*) God! . . . Almighty
God Be . . . (*He stops short. His hands go to his forehead.*)
> *The light dims.*

NOAH: Splash! Did you feel that, my friend? You felt the
first drop! Right on your forehead? between the eyes, as
straight as a die. A perfect shot. (*Savagely.*)

> MAMMA *and the children rise trembling.*

MAN: Oh, you think so? Well, it was a bird – a sparrow.

NOAH: And that?

> *The* MAN'S *hand goes to the back of his neck.*

I suppose that was a nightingale? And that?

> *The* MAN'S *hand covers his eyes.*

A robin, maybe?

> *The* MAN *stretches out his hands and quickly draws them in
again.*

And those. A brace of pigeons?

MAMMA and THE CHILDREN: Oh!

NOAH: Dance, my friend, dance!

> *And the* MAN *dances as if he were trying to avoid a cloud of
arrows.*

Shoot, O Lord! Strike this vile target, pierce it through and
through!

MAMMA and THE CHILDREN (*every hand extended*): It's raining,
raining, raining!

> *Pantomime of the children seeking the rain with every gesture*

around the MAN *whose every gesture dodges the rain. The light
is growing dim.*

NOAH: Pierce the wicked eyes! The prying nose. Those ears.
Seal up those lips and silence that blaspheming tongue.
Pierce the hands that were never raised to You! The feet
that strayed! The glutton's belly and his heart, O God, split
that accursed heart. Shoot, King of Archers, shoot!

　　The MAN *sinks down, still warding off the rain with both
hands.*

MAN: Help! Help! It's burning . . .

　　The light grows dimmer.

MAMMA (*her hands stretched to the rain*): It's cool, cool like the
evening breeze.

THE CHILDREN (*their hands outstretched*): Like the evening
breeze.

MAMMA: Like the blue of the sky.

THE CHILDREN: Like the blue of the sky.

MAMMA: Like the laughter of angels.

THE CHILDREN: The laughter of angels. . . .

THE MAN (*on his knees*): Help me! Help me! Help me! Help
me!

　　Thunder rolls.

NOAH: All aboard! Into the Ark, my good crew! Heavy
weather tonight! Up into our home! Into the ship of God!
You first, Mother, then you, Ada! now Sella! Naomi!
Shem! Ham! Japheth! And we must sing, my children,
come! all together, sing!

　　A clap of thunder.

　　The chorus is singing in unison. NOAH *goes up last. The
storm rages. It is completely dark.*

　　The singing spreads through the Ark.

CURTAIN.

SCENE TWO

In the cabin of the Ark. It is a sort of hut, placed well down stage, in the centre. The light is concentrated on its interior, which is open on the down stage side; above, on the bridge of the Ark, there is rain-soaked darkness. When the curtain rises, MAMMA and the three girls are seen, mending and darning in silence.

MAMMA (*holding up a pair of trousers*): There, that's done. Oh! What a lot of work! I never saw so many holes . . . six weeks. It's disgraceful the way Noah gets through things.

ADA: He has to work so hard.

MAMMA: Yes, poor dear, what a time he has. Six weeks of storms and hurricanes and bad luck! Oh, these dreadful days.

SELLA: And these dreadful nights!

NAOMI: And still it goes on.

ADA: Oh, well, it isn't as bad as it was.

NAOMI: Listen to the rain.

ADA: The rain's nothing compared to the wind.

SELLA: What I hate the most is the thunder. Lying there in my bed, it sounds as if cartloads of empty barrels were going to tumble down on top of me.

MAMMA: Yes, and the lightning. Do you remember that night when there was so much lightning it was like broad daylight? Ada's right though, things aren't as bad as they were.

NAOMI: Just listen to the rain.

Silence except for the drumming of the rain. An animal begins to howl in the hold.

ADA: The lion's worried about something.

NAOMI: That's not the lion.

ADA: Isn't it?

NAOMI: I'd say it was the tiger.

SELLA: It isn't either of them; it's the panther. Isn't it, Mrs Noah?

MAMMA: *I* don't know, dears. All I can tell you is that it isn't the cat. Apart from the cat they all sound alike to me.
   Laughter.

ADA: Oh, Mrs Noah, you're sweet.
   SHEM *comes in from the rear.*

SHEM: Hello everybody. . . . It seems to be raining a bit.
   Pause.

MAMMA: Where are your brothers?

SHEM: Arguing. Exchanging ideas on the situation in general.

MAMMA: And Father?

SHEM: He's taking a reckoning.

MAMMA: Taking a reckoning?

SHEM: That means he's trying to find out where we are.

MAMMA: What do you mean, where we are?

SHEM: What part of the world we're drifting over now.

MAMMA: Drifting? . . . Do you mean the boat is moving?

SHEM: Moving! We're tearing along.

MAMMA: What?

SHEM: Didn't you realize that?

MAMMA: I hadn't the slightest idea! (*Pause.*) I . . . I thought we were floating just about our house. Yes . . . I thought all we did each day was rise a little higher above the house. . . . And – when it was all over – we'd just sink back home again.

SHEM: Oh, no. We must be at least six hundred miles away from home.

NAOMI: Really?

SHEM: Do I look as if I were joking?

SELLA: Six hundred miles!

SHEM: About! Approximately . . .
   Silence. A howl from the hold.

MAMMA: Then – then – we're right out at sea.

SHEM: You're quite right, Mother

MAMMA: Good gracious me! (*She gets up.*)

SHEM: What difference does that make?

MAMMA: Then, down there, underneath us – is the sea?

SHEM: Underneath us, all around us, as far as the eye can reach – all over the world.

MAMMA: And it's – it's waves that make the boat move?

SHEM: Yes, Mother, it's the salt sea waves.

MAMMA: What? Then all this water everywhere . . . is . . . *salt* water?

SHEM: I wouldn't like to swear to it. I've never tasted it, you know.

MAMMA: Is it . . . is it very deep?

SHEM: Incredibly deep, so Father says.

Silence. The beast howls. The three girls begin to cry.

MAMMA: Now, now, children, you mustn't take it like this. At your age, you ought to see the bright side of things.

ADA: I know, but this great big ocean.

NAOMI: This rain —

SELLA: So much water!

MAMMA: Yes, but look at me. I always used to be so afraid of water, that during the rainy season – Noah will tell you – I didn't dare step over a puddle. And here I am in the middle of a puddle so big it hasn't any edges.

Laughter.

All right then. We'll talk and laugh and work and stop worrying about it all.

They go back to their sewing. Voices are heard off stage.

JAPHETH'S VOICE: No, you're wrong. You're all wrong.

HAM'S VOICE: Oh, go on, it's clear as daylight.

JAPHETH'S VOICE: I say you're wrong, do you hear?

HAM'S VOICE: And I tell you I'm not.

HAM *and* JAPHETH *come in at the back.*

HAM: Well, well, how's the mothers' meeting?

MAMMA: Now, Ham! Where are your manners?

HAM: Waterlogged. Like everything else. (*To* JAPHETH.) It's amazing how obstinate you can be.

JAPHETH: I'm not a bit obstinate. I just understand things clearly, that's all.

HAM: Oh, do you?

JAPHETH: Yes, I do.

SHEM and THE WOMEN: Oh, stop it.

HAM: You *see* the hand of God?

JAPHETH: No, I don't see it, but I can feel it. That's the same thing.

HAM: You idiot!

JAPHETH: What did you call me?

THE WOMEN: Quiet! That's enough!

SHEM: If anyone's an idiot, here, I'm the one. Allow me to present the idiot who does all the work while all the loafers stand about and chatter.

HAM: All right, all right.

SHEM: No, it's not all right. I've been minding those animals for a fortnight now, grooming them, feeding them, and putting them to bed! You don't know what that's like.

HAM: I've done it as well.

SHEM: You did once.

HAM: That was enough to find out what it's like.
    Laughter.

SHEM (*laughing*): Lord, what a cheek! (*To* HAM.) You've an awful cheek, you old blackamoor.

NAOMI: I think it rather suits him.

HAM (*laughing too*): It isn't cheek at all. I'm just sensible, that's all. If something bores me, I don't do it. If it amuses me, I jolly well see that no one else does it.

JAPHETH: If everyone were like you . . .

HAM: I know, young shaver, but everyone isn't like me.

MAMMA: Your conceit doesn't seem to have got waterlogged.
. . . Like everything else.

Laughter.

NOAH *appears at the back; there is silence.*

NOAH: Go on. Go on. (*He comes down.*) Enjoying yourselves,
are you?

MAMMA: Yes, Noah. We were having a little laugh.

NOAH: Good, good. I like you laughing, it shows that everything is all right.

HAM: Otherwise you might be beginning to doubt it, mightn't
you?

NOAH (*sharply*): Might I? How about you?

HAM: Oh, so far as I'm concerned . . .

NOAH (*imitating him*): I know, I know . . . you have your own
pet little ideas about the world, haven't you?

HAM: Well, perhaps I have.

NOAH: I know you have.

HAM: Now look here, Father, just one little question . . .

NOAH: I'm only interested in big questions. (*He goes up stage.*)

MAMMA (*going to him*): What is it, Noah? Is something the
matter?

NOAH: No, let me alone, let me alone.

MAMMA: I – I won't; we must share everything, good and
bad, tell us what it is.

NOAH: Perhaps I should have called you – no, no, I think I
was right not to call you. Oh, children, children! Such a
terrible half-hour I have just been through – only a little
while ago – just now, at twilight – just as it was getting
dark, the last people on earth – well, I saw them die, that's
all, yes, imagine – I had to watch them die – those few poor
wretches, huddled together on the top of a mountain, there
they were, that last pathetic little handful of living beings,
and I watched them sinking into the water, one by one.
Such a queer collection too – men and women and some

children – a dog (or a wolf, it may have been, it was too far
off for me to see distinctly) – and a bear – I'm sure it was;
there were some birds too, big white ones, but they flew
away as soon as – oh, well, well, the wind was driving us
along in their direction, and they must have been able to see
us quite clearly, but they never made a sign. They must have
understood, you see. And I felt – oh! if only I could stop
the ship and not go sailing quietly by staring at them. But
what could I do? We drifted on and passed them, quite close
by – so slowly – so terribly slowly – oh children! Children!

HAM: Father, you ought to have —

NOAH: Child, don't you see – there was nothing that I could
do. They never made a sound, just went into the water. Of
course, they knew they could have waited on that mountain
the whole night long, crying for help – no, into the water,
without a word.

ALL: Oh!

NOAH: Do you know what happened then? They started to
swim. Oh! That seemed to me – it seemed so – to watch
them swimming like that – in water twenty thousand
fathoms deep – quietly, carefully, as if there was still hope
– can you imagine it! They swam as if they had hope! Long
before that, the animals, the bear and the other one, had
given up and gone under, in spite of their instinct to pre-
serve themselves. But men keep on swimming – men are
still swimming over this dreadful waste of water. Oh! I
hope, I only hope. He saw it from up there. I hope He saw
it too, that was something for Him to see! – And now
they're dead

Silence.

MAMMA: And we're the only people in the world?

NOAH: I'm afraid so, Mother. I'm afraid we are.

Silence.

ADA: The only ones in the world . . .

NOAH (*gently*): It was bound to happen, you know. The day was bound to come.

NAOMI: All alone, all alone . . . the only ones in the world.

NOAH: Yes, I must say it isn't very cheerful.

SELLA: . . . The only ones . . .

They fall to crying.

NOAH: Now, now, little ones, you knew perfectly well that it was going to happen. It was all leading to this. You must have known.

Silence.

JAPHETH: No, I can't! I simply can't take it in, that's all. The only ones in the world! . . . The only ones? . . . What? . . . Then . . . we'll never see any more people? We're never going to meet anybody again? . . . We'll never . . . never . . . (*He breaks off with a whistle.*)

SHEM (*spellbound*): But all those people we knew . . . all our old crowd, our friends in the village . . . well – it's hard to believe there's no one left. And all the others too . . . the thousands we've never seen, but we knew they existed of course . . . in other villages, in towns, in other countries – all over the world, I mean . . . Pffit? . . . It doesn't seem possible.

MAMMA: Shem, we didn't know many people, really . . .

SHEM: But all the same, Mother, all the same — (*He stops.*) I don't know why I should suddenly think of the postman.

JAPHETH: Funny, I was thinking of him, too.

SHEM: Remember him, Japheth? With his crooked jaw sticking out and his satchel flopping about on his tummy? He was a character, that postman.

MAMMA *sobs.*

And now! The postman's dead, think of that. Condemned to die because of the rottenness of all the rest of mankind, a shameful death for something he wouldn't even understand.

JAPHETH: I know; it hardly seems possible.

    A pause.

HAM: I'll tell you something that's going to seem even more impossible.

JAPHETH: What?

HAM: Sooner or later something will have to be done about replacing all those dead people.

SHEM: What about it?

HAM: Well, my boy, that's where we come in.

JAPHETH: What?

HAM: Who else is there to do it, except us three – and – our three charming companions.

THE THREE GIRLS: Oh!

HAM: Well, damn it all! Unless the Lord begins the work of creation all over again, I don't see how else . . . (*He turns to* NOAH.) Well, Father. How about it? Any ideas?

ADA (*frightened*): Mr Noah!

NAOMI: It can't be true?

SELLA: Mr Noah!

NOAH (*to* HAM): Now then, young man . . . (*He turns to the girls.*) My dear girls, what on earth's the good of making plans about the future? Haven't we enough worries and troubles for the moment? . . . Just be patient. . . . We'll see.

NAOMI: It isn't a matter of making plans; we've got to face the future – look at it squarely. (*Disgustedly.*) Ugh . . . Ha . . . Are we supposed to turn into wild beasts again . . . to behave like animals?

SELLA: Oh, it's all too horrid. It's degrading, that's what it is, simply degrading.

ADA (*pleading*): Mr Noah . . . Mr Noah . . .

NOAH (*to* HAM): Now perhaps you are satisfied?

NAOMI: Well, three boys like these; just three boys; no one else at all, but just these three boys . . . (*To her sisters.*) Just look at them. . . . How's that for the world's supply of husbands.

SHEM: I suppose you think we are any better off?

The boys all laugh.

SELLA (*to* NOAH): And if two of us should want the same one?

NOAH (*never ceasing to smile*): I don't think that will happen.

SELLA and NAOMI: Why not?

NOAH: God wouldn't muddle things like that.

NAOMI: But He doesn't know us. . . . We're — How could He understand us? We're women!

SELLA: What we want is love, and love must choose for itself. Don't you understand?

NOAH: No, I can't say I do.

NAOMI: If you could only make one – one perfect man – out of the three of them! But it can't be done. The tall one is much too skinny, the short one is far too fat, the middle one is neither one thing nor the other. . . . Oh dear, oh dear, oh dear.

HAM (*coming forward*): Anything more?

NAOMI: Don't touch me!

HAM: That's just what I'm going to do. (*He takes her by the arm.*)

NAOMI: Don't touch me! Don't touch me!

HAM: Listen; you're not going to be the ones to choose; *we* are. Just get that into your head. (*He laughs.*) Ha, ha! And to make things easier, how would it be if I chose you straight away, eh? Come on, Naomi, you're booked.

NOAH: Now, now, there's no need to hurry.

HAM (*to* NAOMI): Now I'm going to kiss you.

NOAH: I say there isn't any hurry.

HAM (*kissing* NAOMI *violently three times*): There! There. There.

NAOMI: Oh, you . . . you brute!

NOAH: Now stop it! . . . Ham, let her alone! . . . Oh, you've made her cry.

HAM: I know, for joy. (*To* NAOMI.) Isn't it?

NAOMI (*without conviction*): I hate you.

HAM (*to* NOAH): See? It's joy. Ha, ha, ha.

NOAH: All right, all right, but that's enough. Ham! Do you hear what I say? That's enough, do you understand? Enough. We're all tired, and we've had a hard day. Time for bed now.

SELLA: Bed! . . .

NOAH: Yes, bed, as fast as you can. Things will be better in the morning.

HAM: I don't see what difference the morning's going to make.

NOAH: Well, bless my soul, neither do I! But that doesn't prevent my living in hopes. Good heavens above, do I have to give you lessons in being young? Great Heavens, you're all living in a miracle! Here have you been, seeing nothing but wonders for the last six weeks and now you want to know what is going to happen next. Oh, what babies you all are still! Such babies! But they're good children, really, Mother, they'll turn out all right, you'll see!

JAPHETH: Why don't you ask Him what's going to happen?

NOAH: Oh, certainly, that's a fine idea! I might ask Him the time too, eh! . . . You have a fine idea of God, you have.

He laughs, then the others do too.

JAPHETH: You always tell us He's so simple.

NOAH: Of course He is simple. But that doesn't mean that He's half-witted . . . anyway . . . well, He takes things as they come. Good Heavens, we're alive, aren't we? What more do you want? Now it's time you hopped into bed. Good night, everybody.

THE CHILDREN: Good night, Father.

The family swing their hammocks. HAM *starts to go out.*

NOAH: Where are you off to?

HAM: Just going for a stroll.

NOAH: What on earth for?

HAM: Well, I'm not sleepy.

He goes out.

MAMMA *(going to* NOAH): Good night, Noah.

NOAH: Good night, Mother. (*Then he holds her back and whispers to her.*) Listen, Mother, what do you think about all this? Do you think . . . (*He breaks off.*) Who is that crying?

ADA: I am, sir. . . . Please excuse me. . . . I'll try to stop now.

NOAH: My dear child, whatever's the matter?

ADA: Nothing, sir. . . . Only this rain . . . this rain.

NOAH: But it will stop some day, Ada, dear.

ADA: Are you quite sure, sir?

NOAH: Quite sure. You'll see. Sleep, now, go to sleep and dream about the sun.

ADA: I'll try, sir.

NOAH (*to* MAMMA): Good night, now, Mother. You're all right now, aren't you?

MAMMA: Of course, Noah. Everything's all right.

NOAH (*imitating her*): Of course, Noah, of course. Oh, you old darling. . . . Now go on to bed. It must be almost morning.

MAMMA *kisses him and goes to her bed in a corner. A pause.* NOAH *sits thinking as the rain pours down and the beasts howl below.* NOAH *talks to himself.*

I thought today would never end. It's seemed so long. One felt it wouldn't go unless one gave it a push. Ouch! Well, it's over now. Let me see. . . . That makes exactly forty days! I wonder how many there'll be altogether. Fifty, sixty, eighty? People are funny, always thinking everything will turn out just as they expect – why, I scolded them just now for trying to look ahead, and here I am doing it myself. Well, I suppose I was right to scold them, but it's not so easy when it comes to yourself. Hullo! Now who's snoring? Oh, Mother, bless her heart, and she still says she's never snored in her life. Oh, well, she's tired out, poor thing. They all are, tired and anxious, that's why they squabble and complain. They're good children really, though. Yes, there's nothing wrong with this cargo ... not even Ham. He wants to seem grown-up, that's why he plays the fool. Oh, it's a fine cargo! When we get to harbour, and they're all lined up on the quay – I can see it now – a big white quay all shining in the sunlight – and God says to me 'claim your reward, Noah,' then I'll say to him, 'Lord, all I want is to parade my flock. Look at them: how fine and strong the people are. And how well the beasts are looking. There isn't a pennyworth of disease or wickedness in the whole world. The men are all laughing, and the animals would be laughing too, if they knew how.' And He'll begin to laugh Himself, and He'll laugh so loud He'll knock us all sprawling. Ha, ha.

JAPHETH (*raising his head*): What's the matter? What's the matter?

NOAH: Nothing, son, I was laughing, that's all.

JAPHETH: Aren't you going to bed?

NOAH: Yes, yes, of course ... go to sleep.

(JAPHETH *lies down again and* NOAH *goes on speaking to himself.*)

I can laugh if I want to, can't I? If they won't laugh with me I can laugh just by myself. I don't know why, but I feel as if something good – something gay – were going to happen. I can feel it!

An animal howls.

They feel it too!

More howling.

Something's up. Something's up! (*He gets up.*)

A cock crows.

The cock? The cock? But he's never crowed since —

The cock crows again, waking everyone up. There is much excitement. Above, the day is dawning.

Quiet, quiet, keep quiet. . . . Something's happening. . . .
I'm going to look; wait for me. . . . Stay here quietly . . .
till I look . . .

*He climbs a ladder in a corner, opens a trap-door and goes
through it. The children sit motionless in their beds. Again the
cock crows.* NOAH *appears on deck above the cabin. Quickly the
daylight brightens.*

Why . . . look . . . It has stopped raining!

The sun bursts forth.

My goodness! The sun's coming out! (*He leans over the
cabin.*) Children! Children, come here!

*They all rush to the bridge. The cock is crowing at the top of
his lungs.*

(*Quieting his flock.*) Sh! Sh! Sh! On tiptoe, everybody.
Walk on tiptoe. It's so fresh . . . so young . . . so delicate.

ADA: Look, the deck is steaming.

SELLA: The planks are drying up.

NAOMI: The sea is singing.

MAMMA: The silence . . .

SHEM (*staring at the sun*): A . . . At . . . tchou!

NOAH: Sh! . . . Where's Ham?

JAPHETH: Not here, the silly ass!

NOAH: Ah well, well, well, well. (*Having lined them all up at
the back, steps in front of them and cries in a resounding voice.*)
For . . . The . . . Lord . . . God! King of the Earth! (*He
raises his arm.*)

CHORUS: Hurray! Hurray! Hurray

CHORUS OF ANIMALS (*from below*): Ouahh! Ouahh! Ouahh!

The children laugh.

NOAH: The Golden Age! . . . Just as I said. (*A pause. He gazes
at the sky, the water, the ark, then turns to the chorus and cries
profoundly joyful.*) Good morning, children!

ALL: Good morning, Father!

NOAH: How are you?

ALL: Well!

NOAH: Good!

ALL: And how are *you*?

NOAH: Very well!

ALL: Splendid!

NOAH: Louder!

ALL: Splendid!

NOAH: Louder still!

ALL: Splen-did!

NOAH: That's it! We must breathe, my children, we must breathe. Like this; Ha! We must blow away these forty days of darkness, these forty nights of fear. Our lungs are choked with dust and ashes – blow them away – Ha!

ALL: Hah!

NOAH: Once again!

ALL: Hah-ah!

NOAH: There, we're washed clean. . . . I feel all new inside. In my breast – (*he taps his chest*) – there are white birds all ready to fly straight from my heart to God! . . . Oh, English is a beautiful language. . . . (*He places himself before them, his voice vibrating.*) Walk, children. Let's walk!

    They line up and walk in great strides towards the audience.
To the south, as you see, we have a view of the ocean.

CHORUS (*interested*): Aha!

NOAH (*walking* R.): To the east we have a vast expanse of water, probably salt, of an appearance and character distinctly . . . oceanic.

CHORUS: Well, well!

NOAH (*walking up*): To the north, our prospect opens immediately on to . . . well . . . the sea.

CHORUS: How very convenient!

NOAH: Lastly, to the west we see . . . see and hear . . . the rippling laughter of the waves. (*Towards audience.*) To sum up the entire situation: we are on the water.

CHORUS: We're at sea! Ha!

NOAH: Ha!

CHILDREN: Ha! Ha!

JAPHETH: Faster!

They all walk more quickly.

NOAH: Don't you think it's marvellous?

CHORUS: Marvellous!

JAPHETH: Faster!

Again they quicken the pace.

NOAH: I don't believe Mother can keep up with this.

MAMMA (*panting*): Yes . . . I can! I'm so . . . so happy.

NOAH: No, no, Mother, you needn't keep in line. Just sit out and give us your blessing.

MAMMA (*dropping out*): Oh, Noah! You're . . . so young . . .

NOAH: Young! Upon my soul. I'm as old as the world . . . I was born . . . this morning.

CHORUS: Come on. Faster, faster!

NOAH: On the sea, beneath the sky, between the two great elements as it was in the beginning —

CHORUS (*impatient*): Come on! Come on! Come on! Come on!

NOAH: I give up. (*He drops out and joins his wife.*) But you go ahead. Go on, go on!

THE BOYS: A-Hi! . . . A-Ha! . . . Ah-Yah! Ah-You!

THE GIRLS: You-ou-ou-ou!

NOAH and MAMMA (*sitting on the side-lines beat the measure with their hands*): March! . . . March! . . . March . . . March – march!

CHORUS (*beside itself with joy*): Ha – ah – ah – ah . . . Ha!

They drop in a circle.

ALL: The sun!!

CURTAIN.

SCENE THREE

The deck of the Ark, partially shaded by an awning. The sunlight is intense.

SHEM, HAM *and* NAOMI *are leaning over the rail watching the fish that swim about the Ark.*

NAOMI: There's a beauty! Look at him!

HAM: Grand!

NAOMI: Look at him diving. He is like a paper lantern on a summer night.

HAM: Yes, he is, isn't he? Look, there's the female.

NAOMI: Where, where? . . . Oh, yes, I see her.

SHEM: How do you know it's a female?

HAM: Because it's not as pretty as the other.

NAOMI (*tenderly*): Oh, you pig!

    She embraces him. HAM *turns around; their lips meet.*

SHEM: Now you two. There are plenty of dark corners on this boat for that sort of thing.

HAM: What's the matter, don't you like it?

SHEM: On the contrary, that's just why . . .

NAOMI: Don't you ever kiss Sella?

SHEM: Why should I? Hey, look at those fellows going by.

HAM: Whew! what whoppers! Look, Naomi, look!

NAOMI: All right! I'm not blind.

HAM: What sort of fish are they, Shem?

SHEM: I don't know. Never seen them before.

HAM: But I thought you used to be the finest fisherman in the world!

    A pause.

NAOMI: Why do they all swim two by two?

HAM: Do they? O yes, so they do . . .

SHEM: I don't know. . . . It is funny . . . unless it's because . . .
    (*To* HAM) but you'll laugh at me.

HAM: Never mind, go ahead.

SHEM: Well, don't you think they might be . . . well . . .
    specimens?

HAM: How do you mean?

SHEM: You know. The sole survivors —

HAM: God's own particular pets, eh! Ha ha! That's good.

SHEM: Well, that would explain why there are so many of
    them, and why they go in pairs, and why they've been
    following us for weeks.

NAOMI: They can't come into the Ark, so they just keep as
    close as they can. Ha ha!

SHEM: Well, you find a better explanation, then.

HAM: My dear fellow, we're not expert fishermen; there must
    be some natural explanation. Look at that mass of them!
    The place is alive! Well, doesn't that make your mouth
    water, you old angler, you?

SHEM: Yes, I must say it does rather.

HAM: Well, what about having a shot?

SHEM: What?

HAM (*casting a line in pantomime*): Tchk.

SHEM: Do you think we could?

HAM: Why not?

NAOMI: Oh, do let's!

HAM: Run and rig up a line, Shem . . .

SHEM: But Father —

HAM: O Father my eye! Is fishing forbidden? Since when?

SHEM: Well, I don't believe he . . .

HAM: Ah, you're always in such a funk!

    SHEM *goes towards the back.*

Hurry up, will you? Go on – they're just dying to bite.

>SHEM *goes out.*

I'll burst their little bubble for them.

NAOMI: I knew that you were planning something.

HAM: It isn't the fish that I want to catch . . .

NAOMI (*secretively*): Isn't it really?

HAM: No, my pretty! It's the old man.

NAOMI: Funny, I thought as much.

>*They laugh.*

HAM: Ah, here's the fisherman.

>SHEM *returns with his fish-line.*

To SHEM): Quick work! Good . . . Come on, come on! Here.

(*To* NAOMI): You go and keep cave, my child, do you hear?

NAOMI: Oh, I wanted to watch. . . .

HAM: I'll call you when the fun begins. Come on, Shem. Look, cast here, right in the middle of that bunch.

>SHEM *sits down and throws in his line.* HAM *stands near him;*
>
>NAOMI *mounts guard up stage. A pause.* SHEM *pulls in his line and casts again.*

SHEM: They don't seem to be hungry.

HAM: Give them time, give them time.

SHEM: Hum!

>*Another pause.*

No, they don't seem to bite . . . perhaps we were making too much noise.

HAM: What are we going to do then?

SHEM: Nothing, just wait.

HAM: Oh, go on, Father —

>*A pause.*

NAOMI: Well?

SHEM: Nothing doing.

HAM: There! There! Surely that's a bite?

SHEM: No it's weed.

HAM: Pull in a little and see.

SHEM (*pulling in without result*): Weed!

HAM: I suppose you'll be telling me next there aren't any fish.

SHEM: There are fish all right. They're just not biting, that's all.

HAM: Oh, you and your specimen fish! They're resisting temptation, I suppose.

SHEM: Joke if you like, I bet I'm right.

HAM: Hahaha!

SHEM: Not so loud, you fool! (*He turns.*) See anything, Naomi?

NAOMI: Not a thing. I'll tell you if I do.

SHEM (*to* HAM): Do you know what Father's doing?

HAM: He's down with the animals. They're all he cares about nowadays. He says he understands them. Do you know he even talks to them! Ha, ha!

NAOMI: Look out!

The two fishermen turn their backs to the rail and pretend to chat innocently.

False alarm!

HAM: Good. (*to* SHEM.) Come on, my boy! You're not half trying. There, try for that big one. He's a five-pounder, I bet. Get him by the nose! Quick!

SHEM *casts the line.*

Whew! See him jump. He's biting, isn't he? Go on, strike!

SHEM (*striking without catching anything*): They're not biting, I tell you. Even when their noses are bumping against the hook, they change their minds.

HAM: Go on, try again.

SHEM: I've tried enough.

HAM: Ah, come on, Shem, just once more. One more shot.

NAOMI: Look out! Careful!

HAM (*to* SHEM): Stay where you are! Lean over the side. . . .
  If it's him you can drop the rod into the water.

  ADA *and* SELLA *appear.*

NAOMI: Oh, it's nobody. Only the girls.

HAM: All right, now Shem, come on. One last try. Give it
  everything you've got.

NAOMI: I must be in on this.

  She comes down and leans over HAM'S *shoulder.* ADA *and*
  SELLA *move forward whispering.*

SELLA (*softly to* ADA): Did you hear that? 'Nobody! Only the
  girls.'

ADA: Yes, that's what she thinks these days.

SELLA: Always chasing the men.

ADA: We can clean the dishes and wash the clothes, that's all
  we're good for.

SELLA: All she does is doll herself up.

HAM: Don't whisper like that, kids. It's maddening.

  ADA *and* SELLA *move away a little and continue their*
  whispering.

HAM: Well, Shem, how about it, old boy? Things aren't
  going so well, are they? . . . Well . . .

SHEM: I tell you these fish aren't —

HAM: Oh, shut up! Now go on! fish!

NAOMI: Oh, you darling, you're so wonderful when you
  want something! (*She kisses him.*)

ADA and SELLA: Oh!

HAM (*disengaging himself*): Yes, I know. . . . You keep watch,
  dear, that's all. . . . (*To* SHEM.) Now you listen to me.
  You've got to catch a fish, see? Just one, but I've got to
  have it.

SELLA: A what?

HAM: Shut up! I want to hook something out of the water
  alive so that I can see it wriggle and die before my eyes! Is
  that clear? (*To* SHEM.) Now jump to it!

SHEM *casts again. . . . Silence.* HAM *follows every movement of the line with burning eyes.*

(*Softly.*) That one's showing some interest. Look, isn't he?

SHEM: Perhaps. . . .

HAM: Of course he is! See that he gets a good bite! Careful! One . . . two . . . three . . . strike!

SHEM (*casting in vain*): Blast!

HAM: Damnation! It's no good, no damn good at all. Everything we do, everything we try, it all seems to go wrong. It's all just damn silly nonsense!

SHEM *throws down the fishpole.* HAM *paces the deck in a rage.*

He settles down to sleep. The others sigh. JAPHETH *comes in.*

JAPHETH (*gaily*): Oh, here you are!

NAOMI (*pointing to* HAM): Sh!

JAPHETH (*softly, coming down*): What's the matter?

NAOMI: He's bored.

JAPHETH: Hm. Hm.

He sits down with the others and they talk in low tones.

(*To* SHEM.) Some of the animals don't seem to me to be very well.

SHEM: Did you tell Father about it?

JAPHETH: I couldn't find him. The old tub still not moving?

HAM: Moving! I believe the blasted thing has taken root. Five months it's been like this!

SELLA: Five months.

HAM: That's what I said. Oh, I've kept count all right. Five months of water, of animals, of each other! Five months of waiting – and, my God, we don't even know what for! I tell you it's driving me crazy! And the old man doesn't do anything – he doesn't do a thing – not a single thing.

JAPHETH: What do you want him to do?

HAM: Anything, I don't care! Anything, so long as it'll tire us out and stop us thinking. It's up to him to say what. I don't care how stupid or useless. Why doesn't he treat us like dirt, trample us underfoot?

JAPHETH: You'd be the first to kick.

HAM: Well, and then there'd be some fun, there'd be something to struggle for, something to fight against.

JAPHETH: You can't fight against God.

HAM: Do you mean to say you still – no, you make me tired. Haven't I told you a hundred times —

JAPHETH: Yes, but you haven't convinced me yet.

HAM: Listen, Japheth, Dad's a farmer, isn't he?

JAPHETH: And a jolly good one too —

HAM: Agreed. You probably wouldn't find a better, but still he is only a farmer.

JAPHETH: That's better than being —

NAOMI: Oh, be quiet!

JAPHETH: Who are you talking to?

SHEM: Oh, shut up! Go on, Ham, go on.

HAM: Well, this is what I feel about Father. He's a man of the soil. He understands all about animals and plants and stars and all that sort of thing. He has a sort of instinct for changes of the wind and weather – an amazing instinct – in fact he almost seems to be able to pop in and out according to whether it's going to be wet or fine. He was the only man in the world to foresee that some great catastrophe was going to happen. And so he used his imagination and saved himself and us. But don't you see that all that is only just instinct – it's got nothing to do with miracles. Oh, don't think I'm running him down. On the contrary, it's pretty marvellous. In fact, it's a damn sight more marvellous than calling up God every five minutes for orders. Well, that's what I think, and I don't mind how soon I tell him so.

JAPHETH: If you did it would kill him.

HAM: You can't kill things any more, young feller. That's

what you keep on telling us. How about it, all of you, shall I tell him all that? And a bit more too?

No one speaks.

Don't all speak at once.

SHEM: It's awfully serious, you know. . . . It would put the whole ship in a state of war. And besides . . .

HAM: Well?

SHEM: Well . . . it's no joke.

HAM: All right, my friends, all right! But don't say I didn't warn you.

The BEAR *comes in at the back.*

HAM: Hello, what's he up to? (*He goes to the bear.*) What do you want, you old fathead?

The BEAR *attempts to flee, but* HAM *bars the way.*

No, no, stupid. Not that way. Get in front now, go on.

The BEAR *remains frozen with terror.* HAM *whacks him with his belt. The* BEAR *comes forward and stops among the children.* Get up!

The BEAR *doesn't move.*

Get up, I tell you! (HAM *kicks him in the back.*) Will you get up?

The BEAR *sits up.*

Come on, sit up. Higher. Straighter, hear? More! More! There! Ladies and gentlemen! I have the honour to present the guv'nor's old friend; his favourite pal and confidential adviser. My God! It makes me mad to think of all those fine men and women rotting at the bottom of the sea, while we feed up a brute like this – and all those other beasts down there in the hold. I vote we chuck 'em all overboard. What do you say? And we'll start with you, my lad, do you hear? Well, go on, answer, say something. Chatty, isn't he? Look at him; half a ton of stupid speechlessness. He could talk all right if he wanted to, but he's too cunning. They're all the same, animals; great stupid lumps

with cunning little minds. Look at him! And he hates me.
You do hate me, don't you?

ADA: Oh, don't hurt him, Ham!

HAM: Hurt him! the old wind-bag! Just you wait!

NAOMI: No, Ham, make him dance!

SELLA: Yes, yes, let's have a bear-dance.

HAM: Oh, yes! that's an idea! (*To the* BEAR.) Did you
hear that? All right, get going. One, two! (*He lashes him
with his belt, first one paw, then the other.*) One, two! One,
two!

> *The* BEAR *begins to dance. The children clap their hands and
> chant a sort of melopoeia as an accompaniment, interrupting it
> with bursts of laughter. For a while the* BEAR *dances. Then*
> NOAH *comes in at the back.*
>
> *At first the children do not see him, but the moment he reaches
> them they are abruptly silent. The* BEAR *drops on to all fours and
> moves away to a corner. As* NOAH *gazes at them the children,
> excepting* HAM, *lower their heads one by one.*

NOAH: Not a ripple, not a breath.

> *Meanwhile at the back,* MAMMA *pokes an anxious head out
> on deck, then comes trotting down. She places herself behind*
> HAM, *who suddenly takes a step forward.*

HAM: Father —

NOAH (*firmly*): No.

> *A pause.*

HAM: Look here, Father —

NOAH (*more firmly*): No, I say!

MAMMA (*softly to* HAM): Be quiet, dear, be nice. Don't be
tiresome. . . . Father's busy.

> *Pause.*

NAOMI (*simpering*): Excuse me, Mr Noah, but —

NOAH (*thunderously*): No!

> *He takes a step and the children recoil.*

Go away.

The children mutter, but continue to back up.

Not a word! Off with you! Be off! Get below, everybody!

The children are now all the way up stage.

Who's cabin-boy today?

JAPHETH: I am, Father.

NOAH: Send the animals up on deck. It's past their time.

JAPHETH: Yes, Father.

NOAH: No violence, do you hear? No shouting, or swearing, or beating them. Go along.

The children go away, with MAMMA *following them.*

(*Suddenly tender.*) No, you stay here, Mother. You know I wasn't talking to you. . . . Please stay here with me.

MAMMA: I'd better go with them . . . they want cheering up. (*Her voice is choked.*) It's been a long voyage for them, you know . . . they're not bad, really, Noah. They're not really wicked . . .

She goes away sobbing.

Then NOAH *with a great helpless gesture, sinks down under the awning, facing front. He seems very old and tired. There is a little pause, and then the* LION *appears. He stretches himself and comes down to* NOAH. *The* BEAR *joins him. The two animals lie down at* NOAH'S *feet.*

NOAH: No, don't lie down. . . . Walk about a bit. . . . You must have some exercise.

The animals get up and rest their heads on NOAH'S *knees.*

(*Stroking them.*) Yes, you're good beasts. . . . But don't worry about me . . . I'm just a little tired, that's all. . . . Go along now.

The LION *moves away a little. The* BEAR *rises up and tries a dance step.*

No, Bruin, old boy, no, old boy, don't do that . . . on all fours . . . It's so much better.

The BEAR *obediently drops and goes to join the* LION. *The*

TIGER *comes in, followed by the* MONKEY. *They both want to stay near* NOAH.

Run along. Leave me alone, my friends. . . . Go and play with the others.

The four animals sit up in a row, contemplating NOAH *very sadly.*

(*Deeply moved.*) Leo . . . Sultan . . . Bruin . . . Jacko . . . My friends . . . my friends. . . . (*He weeps.*)

The four animals toss their heads in sympathy. Suddenly the MONKEY *jumps to his feet, calls for attention and begins to dance a hornpipe to amuse* NOAH. *But the* BEAR *trots to him, growling, and pushes him down on all fours with a paw. The* LION *and the* TIGER *approve heartily.*

My friends! . . . My friends! . . .

The COW *comes in, galloping daintily. She nods to* NOAH *in passing.*

(*Drying his eyes.*) Good morning, Daisy, good morning.

The COW *begins to circle the deck, but the* TIGER *bars her way and forces her into line.*

(*His voice trembling, but growing stronger as he speaks.*) It's the children, you see, it's the children. (*The animals nod their heads.*) And then Mother too, she's beginning to give way – she's beginning to fail me. I never knew that happen before. All this happening at once, you know, it's taken me by surprise. It's worn me out, bowled me over. They all keep asking questions: 'Why this? Why that? What now? What next?' Well, I don't know everything, I'm only an old farmer after all. If it was only their natural curiosity . . . because they're young, I mean . . . but it isn't. There's only one thing they're after . . . to catch me out. Oh, my friends, I'm afraid that Ham —

The animals growl.

Now, now, behave yourselves. . . . Yes, I'm afraid it's Ham that —

The animals growl.

He's very unkind to you, isn't he? Well, so he is to me . . .
You've no idea.

The animals are growling louder and louder.

(*Getting up.*) There, there, we mustn't mind. . . . It's all over.
We'll say no more about it.

He strokes the animals and they crowd around him.

And then there is another thing. . . . But mind this is just
between ourselves – between friends, eh?

*He looks about to be sure they are alone, then speaks very
quietly.*

God isn't with us any more. . . . Sh! . . . There!

The animals lower their heads brokenly.

Well, put yourselves in His place. Try to put yourselves
respectfully in His place. Every day, all day long, hearing
His existence doubted, even at times when it is most
apparent. It was all mankind before, now it's these children.
Always asking Him for proofs and miracles; demanding –
ah, it's too much – guarantees! 'If you are God, give us
something else for dinner.' 'If you are God, take away my
toothache.' 'If there was a God, He wouldn't have let
me bang my head coming upstairs this morning.' Yes,
my friends, that was what one of the little girls dared
to say today. So He's gone off on a holiday, you see.
Well, you can't really blame Him, all I can say is it's a
wonder He didn't do it long ago. Goodness knows He's
had patience enough. Well, He hasn't any more, that's
all. After all, He's not a saint, that man. Just think of it,
my friends, God! Almighty God! (*The* TIGER *howls.*) Now,
now, never mind. He'll come back. He's gone to have
a little rest, that's all. He's just shut up shop for two
or three weeks. All right, we'll wait 'till He opens up
again.

. . . . *The other animals howl with the* TIGER.

Sh! Sh! Now – yes, I understand – I know what's the matter. We mustn't give up.

All the animals howl desperately.

Steady! Steady! He'll be horrified if He hears you up there! Call – yes. Call out by all means. We'll all call out together if you like, but not in fear, not in anger. Something that may come sweetly to His ears. Lord! Lord! Now once more, and a good one this time – no shadow of doubt or fear, my children. Lord! Lord! Lord! There, that's enough now. Courage now! Quiet, every one of you. There, there. Rest now. I'm tired, my children. Bruin is going to lend me his back, and I'm going to lie down among you, just the same as you. We'll build a great tower of patience in the midst of the waters, and as the oak tree draws down the lightning, His eyes will light upon it. There, there, we must show Him how well we understand that everything must take time in this world. Hark! The birds are singing. . . . They've not sung for a long time. . . . God is not far off, my children . . .

He sleeps.

The animals lie down, slowly lowering their heads on their paws, and sleep. All is still. A faint sound of wind passes over the stage. The beasts wake up again. The noise of the wind rises again, louder now. The awning begins to flap a little. The animals raise their muzzles to the sky.

CURTAIN.

SCENE FOUR

The deck of the Ark. A great wind is blowing.
As the curtain rises a gale howls over the stage. NOAH *is alone on deck, bursting with delight.*

NOAH: Oh, what a wind! What a wind! Such a fine, splendid wind!
  A gale.
  The waters are sinking – draining away unseen. . . . And good old Mother Earth, buried all this while, comes heaving back to the light with her face washed all clean and shining—
  A gale.
  Bravo, wind! Three cheers for the wind! Oh Lord, many thanks for the wind.
  He sings a sort of triumphal hymn: 'Boom, boom, boom!'
  After a moment HAM *comes in.*
HAM (*interrupting the song*): Father.
NOAH: Ha, ha!
HAM: Father!
NOAH: Eh? (*He turns.*) Oh, it's you. . . . Pretty fine breeze this, isn't it? How about it, my boy?
  HAM *is silent.*
  Isn't it fine, this wind?
HAM (*coming down*): Fine – if only we make use of it.
NOAH: I am making use of it! Listen! (*He sings.*) Boom – boom – boom! (*He breaks off.*) Ham, be a good boy, sing with me. Just a minute, son. (*He tries to take* HAM's *arm.*)
HAM (*pulling away*): Sorry. I can't keep in tune.

49

NOAH: Neither can I. What does that matter?

HAM: Well, *I* don't care to make myself ridiculous.

NOAH: Oh, so I'm ridiculous, am I?

HAM. N-no. . . . No! To do you justice you're so utterly yourself, you are miles beyond being ridiculous.

NOAH: It's nice to hear you say that.

HAM: The pleasure's mine. Look here, Father —

NOAH: Come on now, just sing a duet with me, won't you? It would sound beautiful, I promise you.

> *Gale.*

Oh, just listen to that! Don't you think it deserves a shout of welcome? Come on, Ham, join in. (*He takes his arm, shouting.*) Ha, ha! Ha! Ha!

HAM (*breaking loose*): Let me alone, will you? I tell you I can't – I don't want to.

NOAH: All right, all right. Too bad . . . (*He sighs.*) You want to talk to me?

HAM: I want to ask you something.

NOAH: A favour?

HAM: Advice.

NOAH: Advice! . . . You must be joking.

HAM: Well, it's like this: we – we've been – working below. We've – we've been building things.

NOAH: I thought I heard hammering. Sawing, too. . . . Are you pleased with what you've done?

HAM: I don't think it's bad, but we're not sure it will work. Anyway, we'd like to show it to you. . . .

NOAH: Why yes, with pleasure, come along, let's have a look. What is it?

HAM: Rigging for the ship.

NOAH: Excellent! Splendid! . . . very good! What a good idea. Oh, there are lots of things we could do, lots of im-provements – I've thought about it often. . . . What kind of rigging?

HAM: It's a – well, a sort of – mast. Yes, that's what it is, a big mast.

NOAH (*delighted*): A mast? Really? . . . Oh yes, yes, excellent! A big mast. That will be nice. (*He laughs.*) Ha, ha! . . . How high?

HAM: About twenty feet.

NOAH: You don't say so! . . . You took one of those spare tree-trunks, I suppose?

HAM: We should have asked you first.

NOAH: Yes, of course, of course. . . . Twenty feet! (*He tries to imagine the set up.*) Good for you, carpenters! The old craft is going to look superb!

HAM: We've made a sail, too.

NOAH: Well, I never.

HAM: It's triangular. I cut it out myself. The girls did the sewing, and we used rings off the flour bags for eyelets. The cloth wasn't big enough, so there's a patch in one corner.

NOAH: There's a crew for you! Sneaking away into corners – and then popping up with all sorts of running gear and suchlike! Fancy those girls, too! All those mischievous little fingers scampering over the cloth like busy little ants. Think of that! No, they're not bad at heart, this crew. They're not wicked. Quite possibly it's me after all, who — Well, let's go down and see this business! (*He goes towards the back.*

HAM: And then there's a rudder.

NOAH: Why, you've started a regular shipyard. (*He laughs.*) Ha, ha, ha! . . . A rudder! (*He stops short and turns around.*) A rudder? (*There is silence. He comes back towards* HAM.) A rudder! . . . (*Again there is silence. Then,*) Yes, you are wicked, Ham.

HAM: Now for it! Just as I expected!

NOAH: I should think you did expect it! Yes, you did it on purpose, didn't you? You planned this to bring us face to face – just as we are at this very moment.

HAM: You know, Father, you're not well.

NOAH: You dare to look me in the face and say that?

HAM (*avoiding his eye*): I tell you, you're ill.

NOAH: My poor boy, you're not even wicked, you're just contemptible.

HAM: Look here, Father!

NOAH (*straight at him, through clenched teeth*): You little wretch!

HAM (*the same*): And you – you old —

NOAH (*shouting*): Be silent!

> *Silence.* MAMMA *appears nervously at the back. She does not dare approach.*

You coward! You little coward! Plotting against me. Behind my back! Pretending to be working so hard! . . . a good carpenter . . . with your work bench, and hammer, and saw: using all the things I love so much, just to make a fool of me!

HAM: Oh well, of course if you want to go on drifting about. . . .

NOAH: And so sly he is! So clever! Such an eye for catching people out. . . . Ha, ha. A mast! . . . A big tall mast – set up a beautiful mast! Take the old man up to the top and show him the pretty little rudder!

HAM: Oh, all this fuss about a rudder. . . .

NOAH (*crying out*): Don't you know He's forbidden it?

HAM (*lying*): No . . . I . . . no, I didn't.

NOAH: You didn't know a rudder was forbidden?

HAM: I just said so, didn't I?

NOAH: You didn't know that we must be in His Hands? Helpless as featherless birds in His warm gentle hands? You didn't know we must drift like straws in this great wind He's sent? Or that this boat He made me build was to be nothing but a nutshell on His flood? You didn't know that?

> HAM *shrugs his shoulders without replying.*

Listen to me! Just take that rudder of yours and make

kindling of it. Break it into matchwood – into toothpicks if you'd rather. There's no man living can steer the ship of God!

HAM: That remains to be seen.

NOAH: It's been foreseen! And what's more —

He turns about and goes up stage. HAM *starts to follow.* (*Turning back.*) Stay where you are!

He goes away. MAMMA *comes down to* HAM.

MAMMA: What's the matter?

HAM: Bah! A little argument.

MAMMA: What about?

HAM: I'll tell you later . . . just now there's work to do . . . the great game has begun! (*He rubs his hands.*) Ha, ha, ha. This makes me laugh!

MAMMA: You frighten me.

HAM: Go on, Mother. You've got lots of pluck.

MAMMA: Not so much these days.

HAM: I mean it! You're wonderful. Well, just leave everything to me. Just you trust me and don't fuss. (*He goes up stage, stops and comes back to* MAMMA.) How would you like me to take you to a country where it's warm and mild . . . where the earth is kind, and there's plenty of sunshine . . . where the flowers grow wild, yes, and the vegetables as well? How would you like that, eh?

MAMMA: Oh, my goodness! I'd be so happy.

HAM: All right, just you back me up whatever happens. And you'll have your garden, with a south aspect.

MAMMA: Back you up. . . . Against Noah?

HAM: Well, why not? Can't you understand? He's not in his right mind any more.

MAMMA: But you won't do him any harm, will you?

HAM: Leave everything to me. I'll be back soon.

He starts out and bumps into NOAH *coming in.*

NOAH: Hmph. . . . You'd better go and cheer up your friends

down there. They seem a bit depressed, I can tell you. (*He comes down stage, laughing.* HAM *goes away without a word. Joyfully at sight of* MAMMA.) Hullo, Mother! Oh no, don't run away. Why are you looking so cheerful?

MAMMA *doesn't answer.*

What is it, Mother, won't you tell me? . . . Well? Well?

MAMMA: Why are you always so nasty to Ham?

NOAH: What's that? Why am *I*—? Listen, Mother, you must have made a little mistake. But never mind about that. You just keep out of the argument. Just stay happy and light-hearted, as you've always been.

MAMMA: I'm sorry, Noah, but . . . I can't stand it any longer!

NOAH: Why, what's the matter?

MAMMA: I can't tell you.

NOAH: Well, please try anyway.

MAMMA: This cold wind . . . this icy water . . . my rheumatism . . . your arguments . . . hardly any sleep at night . . . the memories that break my heart . . . is it going to last much longer, Noah?

NOAH: Why, it's over, Mother.

MAMMA: Oh, you always say that.

NOAH: What do you mean 'I always say that'? Do you think I'm making fun of you?

MAMMA: Oh, don't be cross. I only want my house! My house!

NOAH: You shall have it, Mother, I promise you.

MAMMA: When?

NOAH: Very soon.

MAMMA: Yes, but when? When?

NOAH: Well . . . I don't know when exactly.

MAMMA: There you are! You can answer all sorts of odd questions no one would dream of asking. But you can never tell us what we want to know.

NOAH: Oh, come now, Mother, that isn't fair.

MAMMA: I want a house. I can't bear living on this boat any longer, like a gypsy in a caravan. I want a house, with little window-curtains. I want a kitchen full of copper pots. I want a garden full of flowers.

NOAH: Listen, Mother, as soon as the Ark touches ground —

MAMMA: When, Noah, when?

NOAH: Well . . . you see . . .

MAMMA: And what are you doing to make it touch ground?

NOAH: Doing? . . . why nothing . . . I . . .

MAMMA: But if you don't do anything, we'll still be drifting round and round the ocean twenty years from now.

NOAH: What do you want me to do? . . . I've asked God a hundred times.

MAMMA: That's it, you plague Him. You said so yourself. And so He's getting His own back by letting us be battered about on this wretched sea.

NOAH: Please, Mother, don't go on. You'll be saying things in a minute that . . .

MAMMA: You must *do* something, don't you see? Do something practical, like a man.

NOAH: But my dear good woman, what is it you want me to do?

MAMMA: Oh, I don't know; how should I? Couldn't you just ask Ham —

NOAH: What?

MAMMA: He knows! He's capable, he thinks things out. He's a clever boy and he's . . . up to date.

NOAH: Oh, and I'm an old fossil, I suppose!

MAMMA: Oh, no, no, don't you see, you poor dear . . . ? We're a little – you and I, we . . . we date from before the Flood!

NOAH: Oh, but this is too much! This is – this is monstrous!

MAMMA: Of course, if you're going to fly into a temper.

NOAH: Fly! That's just what I am doing! I feel as if I were

flying head over heels above the moon with everything below me upside down!

MAMMA: Good-bye, Noah. We'll talk it over later when you're serious.

NOAH: But I am serious, I promise you!

MAMMA: Do you think I don't know you? You're dying to laugh.

NOAH: Me, Mother?

MAMMA: Yes, you, Father, you. . . . Well, good-bye now. just try to think over what I've been saying.

She goes away.

NOAH (*after a pause*): Ah, well . . . (*Another pause.*) . . . Oh, well . . . (*He sits down on the rail.*) It's too much for me . . . (*Pause.*) What do they want? . . . What in the world do they want? . . . When it rained I asked for sun, the sun came. When we were becalmed – I asked for wind; the wind came. Now I ask for land; land will come. Well then? . . . We have everything! They ought to laugh the whole day long and the whole day long they grumble.

A pause. Indistinctly from below the voice of an orator rises, and outbursts of applause.

Hmph. . . . A mass-meeting in the hold.

Cheers.

Well! Well! What are they up to now?

Again the voice is heard.

Listen to that! . . . Speeches! Arguments! Discussions! (*He raises his eyes to heaven, as if waiting for a word from God. Then he drops his head and sighs.*) Oh . . . men . . . men . . . (*Another little pause, then* NOAH *pricks his ears suddenly.*) What's that? (*He gets up.*) What's that noise? Eh! Eh? What can it be? Oh!

The children enter, all talking at once.

HAM } Come on – now this time settles it.
JAPHETH } But look here, can't we talk it over quietly?

NAOMI: Baby! Baby!

ADA ⎱ He's right – he's right!
SHEM ⎰ Don't all talk at once.

HAM: Very good, I'll do the talking.

JAPHETH ⎱ Of course!
SELLA ⎰ You always do.

HAM: I thought we'd made up our minds that all this non-sense had got to stop!

SHEM ⎱ All right, all right then.
NAOMI ⎰ You know we're all with you.

ADA ⎱ Well, I'm —
HAM ⎰ Come on!

JAPHETH: But —

HAM: Father! We have decided that —

NOAH: Be quiet – quiet all of you — Something is going on down there! Listen to them all down there and running round mile after mile in that small space . . . as if they felt the earth – as if it made them restless. Listen to them tramp-ing!

CHORUS: Ah!

NOAH: In that tramping you can hear the elephants' great pads . . . the little white paws of mother's cat, the buffaloes' hooves, the lions' claws, the tiny feet of the fly.

CHORUS: That's true!

NOAH: The earth is coming back. God told me so. I believe it, but I can't be certain. My five senses that I am so proud of — Ha, ha, not one of them senses earth. But they know everything down there. They're all certain, from the greatest to the smallest. Isn't it amazing?

CHORUS: Yes, yes, it's wonderful!

NOAH: Ham, my boy, honestly, don't you think it's amazing?

HAM: Oh, I suppose so.

NOAH: Let yourself go a bit, like the rest of us. Don't be so calculating all the time. Try it: it will do you good. (*He raises his hands to heaven passionately*.) Oh, God! – you are so – absolutely . . . God! Ada, my child, you are the youngest here. Go and fetch the little white-winged creature, the purest and loveliest of all the animals. Go and fetch the dove.

CHORUS: The dove?

NOAH: Yes, the dove.

NAOMI: Hm! Hm!

CHORUS: Sh!

HAM: You'll spoil the effect.

NAOMI: I'm so excited!

CHORUS: Sh!

> ADA *returns with the dove*.

NOAH: No, no, dear, let it go yourself.

ADA: Oh, I'm not —

NOAH: Just let it go like that, quite easily.

ADA: No, no, Mr Noah, I daren't.

NOAH: Very well, then, give it to me. (*He takes the bird from* ADA's *hands*.)

ALL: Let it go, let it go!

NOAH: Tell me, children, don't you think a nice little prayer would fit into the picture?

ALL: Later, later!

NOAH (*laughing*): Well, well, what a patient family I've got to be sure. All right, then. . . . One, two, three . . . Go!

ALL: Go!

> Silence. Every head is thrown back, watching the flight of the dove in three great circles.

Good-bye! Good-bye!

JAPHETH: Look how she's climbing!

SELLA: The wind's carrying her right up to the sky!

ALL: Yes, yes, straight up!

HAM: Straight into God's mouth.

NOAH: Ssh! Ssh!

SHEM: 'Ware below! The wind's knocking her down! She's falling!

ALL: Falling!

JAPHETH: No, no, no! She's up again!

NOAH: Bravo, little one. Look at her! Look how she's climbing! Climbing the snow-caps, higher and higher, into the distant blue. Bravo, my brave little mountaineer!

SELLA: I can't see her any more.

ALL: Neither can we.

HAM: Perhaps God's eaten her.

ALL: No, no, no, no. We won't listen.

ADA: There she is again!

ALL: Where? Where?

ADA: There where I'm pointing. . . . Higher! Much higher! . . . See that cloud like a horse's head? Well, just beyond that!

ALL: Oh yes!

For a little time everyone gazes up into space.

MAMMA: I can't see her any more. I'm feeling dizzy. There are spots in front of my eyes.

JAPHETH: Now I've lost her myself.

ALL: So have we. We've lost it.

NOAH: She's disappeared.

ALL (*gently.*) Oh! . . .

Silence. The eyes drop from heaven and meet each other. There is general annoyance and the group breaks up. Somebody coughs anxiously. Someone moves about on tiptoe. NOAH, obviously very much moved, goes apart from the others and paces up and down in a dream. HAM, moving aside also, watches the others ironically.

There is a pause. Little groups collect, whispering. The annoyance becomes unbearable. The children, in the centre, begin to swing their gaze back and forth from NOAH, on the right, to

HAM, *on the left. Again there is a pause filled with taut silence.*
Then:

HAM: Well, Father, what now?

NOAH (*from afar*): . . . Eh?

HAM: I said, what now?

NOAH: I don't know what you mean.

HAM: What are we going to do?

NOAH: Well . . . we just wait.

HAM: Ah, we wait? . . . Of course, of course. . . . What for?

NOAH: Results.

HAM: I see, I see. . . . In other words we do just what we've always done.

NOAH: Did you expect a miracle?

HAM: Oh, no. . . . Good Lord, no! I didn't expect anything. But I did expect that you idiots – (*he points to the children* – wouldn't let yourselves be fooled by him for the hundredth time.

SHEM: But listen, old boy, you didn't say anything, so we . . . How were we to know?

HAM: He's caught you, my little pets; he's caught you again.

SHEM: He tells us to watch something, well, we watch it, that's all.

HAM: Yes, and you don't see anything, but you're quite happy all the same.

SHEM: You must admit that all that business with the dove was rather fun.

HAM: Killingly funny, I must say.

SHEM: I don't mean that, I mean —

NOAH: Ah, good heavens, are you going to start arguing all over again? Well, go somewhere else to do it.

HAM: I beg your pardon. We've finished arguing. Quite finished! Completely finished! You can take your authority, your absolute power, your divine right – and all the other

relics of the past – and make matchwood of them – or toothpicks, if you'd rather.

NOAH (*taking a step towards* HAM): What did you say?

HAM: You heard what I said.

NOAH: Listen to me!

HAM: I won't listen.

NOAH: Be off at once, for the last time. I order you, do you
hear?

HAM: I won't!

THE OTHERS: We won't!

NOAH: You young puppy, you're asking for a thrashing, and
you needn't think that you're too old for me to give it to
you.

HAM: I'll see you damned first!

MAMMA (*throwing herself between them*): Stop! . . . You're both
mad! Don't! Don't! Go away! Please! Stop! (*With all her
strength she pushes them apart.*) Lord, isn't the world big
enough to hold the pair of you!

HAM: The world, probably, but not this boat . . . certainly
not this boat.

NOAH: Then get off it!

HAM: Why don't you get off it yourself?

NOAH: You young cub!

HAM: Oh, don't get excited. You know I didn't mean that
literally. All I want you to do is to give up your command,
that's all.

NOAH: Oh, that's all, is it?

HAM: I demand this in the name of every one of us.

NOAH (*to the children*): Is this true?

SHEM: Listen, Father —

NOAH: I asked you, is this true?

SHEM: Well, yes.

THE OTHERS: Yes.

NOAH: Is this true, Mother?

SHEM: Father, you must understand.

NOAH: Be quiet, you! . . . Is this true?

MAMMA (*very softly*): Yes, Noah . . . yes, Noah.

> *Silence.*
>
> NOAH *goes up stage a little, stops for a moment, his back turned. Then he comes back smiling to the children.*

NOAH: Now, look here, children – don't you think you could make just one more little effort to try again?

HAM: Impossible, out of the question!

NOAH (*to the children*): You know I don't care a bit about my command. Only, over me – good heavens, there's God!

HAM: Oh, always God.

NOAH: Why, He was talking to me only this morning. You've no idea how kind He is to me. He's changed so much lately – and for the better, you know. Not less tremendous, of course, but nearer, less remote. He joked a bit – at least. He pretended to be joking to hide His real feeling, but I've a pretty keen ear, you know, and I could hear His great voice shaking with emotion at finding us again. So how could you have the heart . . .

HAM: No, no, stop! . . . That's enough . . . stop it! Those old tales again! . . . You're as cunning as a serpent. (*He turns to the children.*) Wake up! Wake up! Don't believe him, it's not true. Why, the old man's telling you fairy tales – throwing dust in your eyes. It's nothing! Nothing at all! Come on, are you with me?

THE CHILDREN (*hesitantly*): Yes . . . yes . . .

NOAH: Listen to me!

HAM: Not another word! (*To the children.*) We're banded together, comrades! Together! Remember all we've said, all we've agreed together was good, and true, and real! Do you remember?

THE CHILDREN: Yes!

HAM: Remember it all?

THE CHILDREN: Yes! Yes!

HAM (*to* NOAH): We don't believe you any longer. We don't believe the pretty fairy tales that drop from heaven.

THE CHILDREN: No, we don't!

HAM: We only believe in the truth that we know ourselves.

THE CHILDREN: That's right! That's what we believe!

HAM: We want to live! We want excitement and adventure. We want to make discoveries and risk dangers. What's the good of humility and prayer and contemplation – that's all just cowardly laziness. We want to live!

THE CHILDREN: That's what we want!

HAM: Forward! Forward! Set up the mast! Hoist the sail – our fine big sail. We'll catch this wind and head straight for the south, rolling with the ship, singing with the ship, laughing as we know how to laugh!

THE CHILDREN: Hahaha! Come on, come on!

They break into chant, and rush away to get the mast and the sail. MAMMA *remains alone.*

NOAH: And where do you think you are going, you young fool?

HAM: Somewhere there must be land – cities – people – crowds of people – that never saw your flood! All over the world there are men who won't even believe all this when we tell it.

NOAH: That's not true.

HAM: I know it is!

NOAH: It's not true! It's not true!

HAM: It is true! I feel it! We all feel it! Come on, forward!

THE CHILDREN (*returning*): Forward! Forward!

They raise the mast, singing.

NOAH: You can't! You can't! It's wicked!

HAM: I'll take the blame.

THE CHILDREN: So will we!

The mast rises.

NOAH: Stop! Wait! I beg you only to wait until the dove comes back!

HAM and THE CHILDREN (*laughing*): Hahaha! The dove —

NOAH: We must wait for the little creature! That's all I ask. If she doesn't find us here when she comes back —

HAM: She won't come back!

NOAH: Won't come back?

HAM: Of course not, old boy. She's drowned.

>   *Laughter from the children.*

HAM (*to the children*): Come on, hurry! We've a long way to go. We must get started before dark.

THE CHILDREN: Aye, aye, Captain!

HAM: Oh, this is going to be a glorious trip!

THE CHILDREN: Hurrah! Hurrah!

>   *The sail unfurls.*

NOAH: Oh, my poor old boat! (*To the children.*) Stop! Stop! No! No! Don't trim the sail! Oh! Just a little, please, please — (*He runs to the foot of the mast.*)

HAM: Get back, Father! Back!

NOAH: Think! Think a minute, I beg of you! Don't . . . don't – don't force the Ark of God into the channels of Mankind! It's free! Let it be free!

THE CHILDREN: Keep back! Keep back!

NOAH (*clinging to the mast*): No. You can't do it! You haven't the right! You mustn't do it!

HAM: Look out, Father! . . . Get out of the way!

NOAH: I won't budge! I won't move! I stay here!

HAM: Seize that man and lock him up below!

>   SHEM *and* JAPHETH *rush at* NOAH. *Just as they come to grips,* MAMMA *shrieks suddenly.*

MAMMA: Here it is! Stop! Look! Here it is! Look here!

THE CHILDREN: What? . . . What? . . . What?

MAMMA: The dove. It fell straight from heaven into my hands.

HAM: That's a lie.

MAMMA: I swear it!

HAM: It's a lie!

NOAH (*hitting him with all his strength*). Perhaps you will believe that! Well, come on, who's next?

    Silence. MAMMA *goes to* NOAH, *kneels before him and offers him the dove.*

NOAH: Now, Mother, come, come . . . get up.

MAMMA: Oh no, Noah, please let me stay like this. . . . Oh, Noah, I'm not worthy.

NOAH: Now, now . . . (*He lifts her up.*) Ah! . . . Why can't we all be simple-hearted? . . . (*He strokes the dove.*) It wasn't hard, was it, my pet, to do your little bit to help, and now all's well! Look, Mamma, see how well she is . . . warm . . . happy . . . cooing . . . she's cooing here in my hands . . . and look. . . . What has she got in her beak?

    The children come nearer.

A little leaf . . . three little leaves . . . a little green twig!

THE CHILDREN (*very softly*): A little green twig!

NOAH: What's the name of it, Mother? You know all the plants.

MAMMA (*drying her eyes*): It's . . . an . . . olive branch.

NOAH: An olive branch.

THE CHILDREN: An olive branch.

NOAH: The trees are above the water.

THE CHILDREN: Hoo! . . . Hoo! . . . Hoo! . . .

HAM: Above the water?

SHEM and JAPHETH (*slowly*): Above the water!

THE GIRLS (*quickly*): Above the water!

ALL OF THEM (*loudly*): Out of the water! (*They begin to tremble violently.*) Haa! . . . Hoooo! . . . Out of – the waters! Out of – the waters! (*More quickly.*) Out of the waters! (*They run towards the hold.*) Out of the waters! Out of the waters! *They disappear screaming. There is a pause.*

MAMMA: It's happened . . . just as you said it would.

NOAH (*without any joy*): Yes.

MAMMA: Everything's happened just as you said.

NOAH: Yes.

MAMMA: Just as you said.

NOAH: Yes, Mother.

MAMMA: Just as you said. . . . Just as you said!

NOAH: Please don't, Mother.

Below there is an explosion of glee. Shouts, songs, a sound of an accordion mingle.

Ah! Even this moment – they destroy it!

Shouting and pounding from the hold.

Bunglers! Ruining everything you see; spoiling everything you touch! Bunglers.

A perfect din rises from below.

Spoiling joy! Spoiling youth! Spoiling happiness!

The din grows louder and louder.

Oh Lord, Lord! Old Friend. . . . It's all a failure! Everything's a failure! Kick the lot of us overboard and say no more about it!

He drops his head on MAMMA'S *hair, sobbing.*

CURTAIN.

SCENE FIVE

The top of Mount Ararat. The Ark is to the left. Only the bow is visible, with a ladder to the ground.

The animals are grouped in the centre of the stage. They take a last look at the Ark, and exit in various directions.

NOAH *comes down the ladder, alone and silent. He descends the last rungs slowly, places one foot on the ground, then the other, and kneels.*

A pause. MAMMA *enters on the Ark.*

MAMMA: There now. I'm quite ready. I arranged a basket for the cat. She'll be very comfortable. It's like a little house. (*Then she is gloomy.*) But she won't want to stay in it. She scratched me. Then she jumped out of the basket. All the animals have gone wild again and they're making her wild, too. Oh, children, children, what a shame, what a shame.

She weeps. NOAH *gets up and crosses to up stage. The* LION *and the* TIGER *howl in the distance.*

Oh, what a desert place! So cold. So bare. So bare! And this horrible smell of stagnant water. Why is it all so cold? Noah! Where are we? Where's the water? Where's the ocean? . . . I'm frightened. Oh, I was getting a basket ready for the cat. . . . Kitty! Kitty! Come here, dear, you're all I have left.

She goes back into the Ark. NOAH *coughs. The* LION *is heard again in the distance. Suddenly all the children throw their bundles to the ground and jump off the Ark.*

ALL: Ah!

THE BOYS: Aha!

THE GIRLS: Haha!

They are all lined up before the Ark.

HAM: Ha! Old Earth!

THE BOYS: Good old Earth!

THE GIRLS: Dear old Earth!

JAPHETH (*stepping out of line*): Look! I'm going to walk! Watch me walk! (*He takes a step.*) What am I doing?

ALL: Walking!

JAPHETH (*slapping his chest*): What's this boy doing?

ALL: He's walking!

JAPHETH: Walking where?

ALL: On the ground!

NAOMI (*getting out of line*): Look at me! Look at me! (*She pulls her skirt up to her knees.*)

ADA and SELLA (*copying her*): Look at us.

NAOMI (*tapping the ground*): I'm squelching in the mud.

ADA and SELLA: We're squelching, too.

THE BOYS: Let's all squelch. (*They do so.*)

HAM: It's wet!

JAPHETH: It's cold!

SHEM: But it's warming up under our feet.

THE THREE BOYS: It's soft! It feels so good!

ALL: One, two! One, two!

NAOMI (*with a shrill laugh*): Look! My feet are all black!

ALL: One, two! One, two!

HAM (*getting out of line*): Be quiet!

ALL: One, two!

HAM: Shut up! Shut up! (*Pause.*) I want to feel that at last – I'm really *free!*

　　All are silent.

　　(*Stretching.*) Nobody. (*Louder.*) Anybody here?

　　　NOAH *coughs.*

ALL: Sh!

HAM (*shouting*): Ham! . . . Me! . . . I . . . (*He climbs a little hill, centre.*) Ham!

NAOMI (*pulling her sisters*): Let's go and look!

ADA and SELLA (*they run up stage*): Let's look at everything.

NAOMI (*glaring at Ark*): Boo! Boo! That old wreck!

ADA: Rotten decks.

SELLA: Rusty nails!

ALL THREE: Boo! Boo! Boo!

They spit on the Ark.

HAM (*from his height*): Ham is on top of his world.

JAPHETH (*climbing up*): Here comes Japheth.

HAM: No, you don't.

SHEM: Shem's coming too!

HAM! Neither Japheth *nor* Shem! (*Planting himself firmly, he keeps them off with both hands.*)

NAOMI (*up stage*): We're on a mountain.

ADA and SELLA: High mountain.

The three girls separate. SELLA *goes down right,* ADA *up centre,* NAOMI *down left. Meanwhile* SHEM *amd* JAPHETH *shout and attack the hill from opposite sides.*

HAM (*driving them off*): No! No! No, you don't.

SHEM and JAPHETH (*slipping*): Why not?

HAM: I climbed up first. I got here first! I'm the strongest.

SHEM: I'm the oldest.

JAPHETH: Well, I'm the youngest.

They come to blows. NOAH *watches without saying anything.*

ADA: Look at the water! It's streaming down the mountain in little rills.

SELLA: The animals are streaming down after them.

NAOMI: Everything's streaming down. They're all going down.

ADA: There are plains already.

SELLA: There's a jungle, too.

NAOMI: And deserts, too.

The boys are fighting.

THE GIRLS (*running towards them*): No!

JAPHETH (*to* HAM): Black man! Blackamoor! Nigger!

SHEM (*to* JAPHETH): Baby! Cissy! Pale face!

HAM (*to* SHEM): Yellow! Yellow skin! Chink!

They roll down the hill and start up again. But their wives cling to them.

NAOMI: No, no! Why fight over a little lump of rock when the world is so wide.

SELLA: The world is all around us.

ADA: There it is! Down there!

THE THREE GIRLS: Down there! Down there!

But the boys free themselves and go back to their fight.

JAPHETH (*to* SHEM): Chink! Slant-eyes!

HAM (*to* JAPHETH): Pale-face! Whitey!

SHEM (*to* HAM): Nigger. Blackamoor!

They roll down the hill again. The girls pick them up and hold them fast.

NAOMI (*to* HAM): Behind you, Ham! Look behind you. Southward. Southward! Look straight into the south. Come. Come, my hunter. Follow the lion over the sands to the south!

SELLA (*to* SHEM): To the East! To the East! After the tiger! We'll ride an elephant through the jungle, where monkeys chatter as we pass. Come, my peasant!

ADA (*to* JAPHETH): Come, my shepherd. Take up your pipes. We'll follow the cow and the sheep and the dog into the mists and valleys of the west. Come, my shepherd.

The three panting boys each turns in his own direction.

THE GIRLS: Come!

NAOMI: All life has gone down the mountain.

The boys start to follow the girls, then suddenly turn and embrace.

THE BOYS: Good-bye!

THE GIRLS: Come!

They run and gather up their bundles. NAOMI *struggles up with hers and* HAM'S *and puts them on her head.* SHEM *loads his on his shoulder.* JAPHETH *and* ADA *put theirs together and carry them between them.*

THE GIRLS: Well. There.

THE BOYS: There!

They all look at the Ark, then at NOAH. NOAH *is on his knees, up right.*

ALL: Sshh! (*softly.*) Farewell.

They go away, NAOMI *before* HAM, SHEM *leading* SELLA, JAPHETH *and* ADA *side by side, and disappear down the roads they have chosen.*

A shepherd's pipes are heard. A pause. NOAH *gets up and turns fearfully to the deserted stage.*

NOAH: They've all gone down the mountain. . . . Every living thing. What of me, my children? I'm alive! (*He calls.*) Children! Children! You've left someone behind! . . . You've forgotten someone!

The pipes grow more distant.

It isn't possible. Surely they can feel me willing them to turn their heads. I can't believe that you'll look straight before you without a thought. You will come back, won't you? You'll come back sometimes at least. In your hearts you cannot really feel content – it isn't possible. You're my flesh and blood. Something still binds you to me like a cord. It must be wrenching at you, straining, pulling you back to your poor old Father. Isn't it? Isn't it? Shem, old chap – Japheth, my child, Ham, Ham, my boy.

The pipes stop.

Ah! ah! ah! It's all over – I can't hear them any more. Help! Help! I can't follow them, I can't go with them – which way? which way? They've bound me, fenced me round, shut me up in nothing. I'm caught in the midst of nothing. All! Hark, there they are. I can hear them again – their steps, little footsteps in the distance. Ah, tell me I still hold

fast the reins of my three splendid teams . . . Shem and
Sella . . . Ham and Naomi . . . Japheth and Ada! . . . Steady
there, steady. (*He kisses the ground.*) Oh, the reins are slipping
– they're stretched to breaking point – they're snapping!
Oh, my children, catch up my voice as it flows to you
through the earth in three fresh streams. Take one last
drink. . . . (*He stops, places his ear to the ground and then gets
up. His voice is cold and dead.*) Gone over. Finished . . . very
well! (*He sighs and beats his breast.*) How's the heart inside,
then? My blood! The old lungs! You must make plenty of
noise and work hard, to keep me company. (*He surveys the
scene, laughing despairingly.*) Ah! Ah! Ah! Ah! I think I'll
have to raise an echo, a fine, deep echo – so that I and myself can have a bit of a talk! (*He cries.*) Noah! Noah! (*He
listens.*) Nothing!

　　Enter the BEAR.

Well, if it isn't Bruin. This *is* a surprise. D'you know you
couldn't have turned up at a better moment! I thought
you'd left me, too. . . . Oh, I'm delighted to see you again.
. . . I always thought we had a little weakness for one another. (*He goes towards the* BEAR, *who stands up.*) Yes, you
understand all sorts of things.

　　The BEAR *opens his arms.*

What? Come on then, give us a hug. Good old comrade!
(*He goes into the* BEAR'S *arms.*) Dear old friend! Oh, I say!
He's squeezing hard! . . . Oy, there, you're hugging me so
I can't breathe! . . . Here, steady, old man! Oof! . . . You're
smothering me! Let go, do you hear? Let go! Heah! High!

　　His voice is muffled in the BEAR'S *fur. Man and Beast
struggle in silence.*

NOAH (*throwing back his head*): Help! Help!

　　MAMMA *appears on the Ark.*

NOAH: Help!

MAMMA (*bursting into laughter*): Hahaha!

NOAH: Mother!

MAMMA: Hahaha!

>NOAH *succeeds in getting free, gets his wind and rushes shouting at the* BEAR, *who scampers away.*
>
>NOAH *pants and mops his brow.*

MAMMA: That was funny! That was so funny!

NOAH: It nearly killed me, Mother.

MAMMA: Dancing together like that. A real bear-dance. Ha, ha, ha. (*She roars with laughter.*) Tra la la, tra la lee, I kiss you, you kiss me – ha, ha, ha, ha!

NOAH (*raising his eyes to heaven*): There's the vulture already. It will take a lot of courage.

MAMMA (*squatting down stage, her chin in her hands*): Where are the children?

NOAH: They'll be back soon. They've gone to look round a bit now that things are coming back down below. But they'll be back here soon. They'll come back in a few days.

MAMMA: It's very strange that none of our friends have taken the trouble to come and see us.

NOAH: What friends, Mother?

MAMMA: Well, our friends in the village. My personal friends. Of course, nobody liked you. But I had a lot of relations. After a trip like this you'd really think they might have called.

NOAH: But, Mother. . . .

MAMMA: What? . . . Has that been forbidden, too?

NOAH: No, no! . . .

MAMMA (*getting up*): It's Him up there! . . .

NOAH: No, no. . . . You mustn't say that!

MAMMA: Somebody's got to say it. I'm not afraid to tell Him what I think. I'm not mad, you know. (MAMMA *sobs softly.*)

NOAH: Sit down, Mother. There, there, there. I want you to help me choose a nice place for our new house. You know I'm going to build you a brand new house. There's plenty of wood here. You're going to have that wonderful, enormous kitchen you've always dreamed about.

MAMMA (*weeping*): I'm cold.

> NOAH *takes off his coat and puts it around her.*

MAMMA: What's that falling on my hair?

NOAH: A little snow, maybe.

MAMMA: Snow?

NOAH: Yes. . . . Ah! . . . How shall I begin? (*To* MAMMA.) Are you all right?

> MAMMA *makes no reply. She is falling asleep.*

She's asleep, poor old comrade. She couldn't hold out . . . till the very end. Yes. (*Softly.*) It has been hard. . . . (*Louder, and shaken with sobs.*) It certainly has been pretty hard! . . . It's a good thing I have such trust in You. . . . Do You hear? I'll say You've given me some pretty hard knocks. It's been a bit past a joke sometimes, I can tell You! You take me from my garden and chuck me on a bare rock, all by myself, with a hundred ways of dying. . . . Haha! . . . All right, all right. Don't You worry. I'll find a way out, somehow or other. I'll find a way out all right! I tell You frankly I've given up trying to understand. But no matter. Go on, I'm following You! Oh, let's go on! Only just one thing I'd like to ask You. Be up there a bit just now and again, will You? Just let me hear Your voice once in a while, or feel Your breath, just see Your light, even. Lord, if You'd just shed Your light on my work as I do it every day, and give the *feeling* – *the assurance* – the conviction that You are satisfied. We must all be satisfied, mustn't we? (*He attacks the Ark with his hatchet.*) Well, I am satisfied. (*He shouts.*) I am satisfied! (*He sings.*) Are You satisfied?

> *The seven colours of the rainbow appear in the background.*

That's fine!

CURTAIN.